Sara Jeannette Duncan

SELECTED JOURNALISM

# Sara Jeannette Duncan

# SELECTED JOURNALISM

Edited by
## Thomas E. Tausky

The Tecumseh Press Ottawa — Canada
1978

© The Tecumseh Press Limited 1978

ISBN 0-919662-55-2

The Publishers gratefully acknowledge the support of the Canada Council and the Ontario Arts Council.

The Tecumseh Press Limited
8 Mohawk Crescent
Ottawa, ONT., K2H 7G6
CANADA

Printed and bound in Canada.

# Table of Contents

*Title supplied by the editor

## IV: CITIES

## V: INSTITUTIONS

## VI: LITERATURE

---

*Title supplied by the editor

# General Introduction

Sara Jeannette Duncan regarded her own strong ambition as a natural product of the age in which she lived. "In this golden age for girls," she begins an autobiographical essay, "we all want to do something; something more difficult than embroidered sachets, and more important than hand-painted tambourines."

Sara Jeannette Duncan did indeed do something. Many Canadian women in the 1880s may have shared her desire for self-expression, but her achievement is unique. She wrote editorials, book reviews and columns at an astonishing rate for newspapers in three countries. She eventually wrote eighteen novels, a travel book, a book of short stories, a half-fictional autobiography and several full length plays. The relentless application of pen to paper is, of course, no guarantee of literary immortality; however, Sara Jeannette Duncan's enormous output includes much journalism and fiction that is still of interest today.

She was born in Brantford, Ontario, in December 1861. Her father had emigrated from Scotland a few years before, and soon established himself as a successful merchant and prominent citizen. Sara's ambition as a girl was already "to distinguish herself in literature," but for a short time she apparently took up the more conventional profession of school-teaching. She persisted, nevertheless, in efforts to plot a strategy for literary success. In the fall of 1884, she managed to persuade a few newspaper editors to let her submit articles for their consideration on the New Orleans Cotton Centennial, the World's Fair of its time.

After that task was performed with great success, Sara Jeannette Duncan could not be stopped. A year later, she was writing editorials for the Washington *Post*. By July, 1886, she was writing a daily column for the Toronto *Globe*. In 1887, she decided to work for the Montreal *Star*, and within a few months her editors there sent her to Ottawa as a parliamentary correspondent. By 1888, her enthusiasm for travel took her around the world; the reports she wrote for the *Star* and other newspapers later became the basis for her first book, *A Social Departure*.

The trip also changed her life. In Calcutta, she met Everard Cotes, then a museum official, and subsequently a journalist. After marrying Cotes in 1891, she spent most of the next three

1

decades in India, with extended visits to Canada and England.

After 1890, Sara Jeannette Duncan concentrated on fiction. In the middle 1890s, however, she combined a steady flow of novels with considerable editorial writing for the *Indian Daily News*, a Calcutta newspaper edited by her husband. Her best fiction was written between the early 1890s and 1910; her efforts at becoming a playwright and her last novels indicate a sad decline. She died in 1922, shortly after moving into a new home in Surrey.

It took determination, which Sara Jeannette Duncan had in massive quantities, for a woman to establish herself in journalism in the Canada of the 1880s (see the article "Women in Journalism" reprinted below). Following the familiar Canadian pattern, Sara had to prove herself in the United States before she got her chance on *The Globe*; she was also the first woman to be hired on a full-time basis by that newspaper. But once she was given a job, her editors granted her (or perhaps she simply took) remarkable freedom in choice of subject. Many readers of *The Globe* must have been startled by her feminist tendencies, just as some readers of *The Week*, that culture-conscious journal, were surely dismayed when informed that "Ontario is one great camp of the Philistines."

Perhaps it was the charm of her prose style that enabled her to express her audacious views without editorial interference. By means of stylistic devices such as abrupt beginnings, facetious circumlocutions and confiding appeals to the reader, she made her opinions seem simply part of a daring, forthright personality. There are times when she falls into the journalist's sin of striving for cleverness at all costs, when an unusual expression seems merely strained and affected, but for the most part her method wins attention and sympathy. Ninety years later, her distinctive, witty voice speaks casually but compellingly to us, telling us what it was like to be young and successful and gay and emancipated in Victorian Canada.

I have tried to make this collection as representative as possible of Sara Jeannette Duncan's interests. Selections have been chosen from five newspapers, *The Week*, and *A Social Departure*. I have regretfully omitted parts of some articles in order to have the space to reprint others; omissions are indicated in the customary way by three or four periods. For the sake of easier reference, I have dared to invent individual titles for those selections which originally had only general headings such as "Woman's World" (*Globe*) or "Bric-a-Brac" (*Star*). Within sections, the articles are in chronological order.

Further remarks on Sara Jeannette Duncan's journalism may be found in the introductions to the various sections of this anthology, and in my full-length critical study of the author, which is scheduled to appear within a few months of the present work. I am grateful to the Canada Council for a grant which enabled me to buy microfilm of the *Indian Daily News*, and to the National Library of India for supplying that microfilm. Rae Goodwin's excellent thesis, "The Early Journalism of Sara Jeannette Duncan," first aroused my interest in the subject, and Mrs. Rae Storey (as I have known her) has been a very helpful and gracious correspondent. My wife Nancy gave valuable advice on the choice of selections.

# I    Autobiography

**Introduction**

"How an American Girl Became a Journalist" is the closest thing we have to an autobiography of Sara Jeannette Duncan's earlier years. If Margery Blunt went to Quebec City and New Orleans, so did Sara Jeannette Duncan, as we know from other articles she wrote. There is no reason to doubt that in essentials this essay presents accurate information as well as sincere self-evaluation.

Miss Duncan's analysis of the process that led to her success is more complex than may appear at first sight. A key element, in her view, was the acceptance of her very early article on Quebec; she was thereby encouraged to discard moralizing in favour of the lively narration of personal experience. Her next logical step was in the direction of the nearest newspaper office. The opportunity to go to New Orleans, which led immediately to further successes, is seen as the tactical means of achieving recognition, rather than as an experience that totally transformed her literary and personal outlook. By the time she came to write "How an American Girl Became a Journalist," Sara Jeannette Duncan had reason to feel that her early ambition, her eventual choice of an appropriate subject and style, and her determination to make opportunities for herself had each contributed to her deliverance from home-town obscurity.

Sara wrote about New Orleans for the Washington *Post*, the Toronto *Globe*, the London (Ont.) *Advertiser* and the Memphis *Appeal*. Her articles were shrewdly observant and (proof of her own self-assessment) assured in manner right from the start. She made two exotic side-trips from New Orleans—a visit to British Honduras as a guest of the Governor, and a trip to Florida in search of the Fountain of Youth. She evidently regarded the latter excursion as highly significant, since she chose to describe it several times. The version reprinted here is quite characteristic, in that it combines moral earnestness (in her praise of the Chautauqua Movement) with a joyous delight in life (in her account of Ponce de Leon's transformation, and its setting). Ponce himself, if we must shatter a romantic illusion, was Joaquin Miller, a poet of some reputation whose talents seem to have been largely in the field of self-publicity.

## How an American Girl Became a Journalist

In this golden age for girls, full of new interests and new opportunities, we all—you, the musical girl; you, the literary girl; you, the artistic girl; you, the practical girl; and I, whose appropriate adjective is of no consequence—want to do something; something more difficult than embroidered sachets, and more important than hand-painted tambourines. The sachets and the tambourines are very charming in their way, but as the chief industrial end of life we have begun to find them unsatisfying.

Girls in America seem to be even more convinced of this than girls in England, judging from the enterprise with which they act upon the conviction. Margery Blunt, for instance, is an American girl, and I fancy what she did by way of replacing the sachets and the tambourines in her life was new to her English friends when they heard of it, and may be new to you.

I knew Margery Blunt well—very well indeed. I knew her before she became a journalist, when she lived largely in a corner attic of her father's home in the society of three spiders, two mice, the family medicine chest, her grandfather's hat-box, and a Secret Purpose—which is the beginning of this history—and I have known her ever since. So that I think I may give you this account of her experience as strictly and entirely true.

Margery's Secret Purpose was to distinguish herself in literature. She told herself, with a great show of candor, that she knew she was not a genius, but she had privately picked out two or three names of modest fame in the lighter arts of the pen, whose achievements she thought she might reasonably hope to parallel in the course of time. Margery was not altogether without provocation to a purpose of this kind—people very seldom are. At school her essays had a clever facility which interested her teachers, and suggested to numbers of her fellow-pupils that she should inspire theirs also. Besides which, she absorbed the spirit of every artistic thing she read so thoroughly that for the moment she was almost ready to exhale something very like it with all the pride of conscious originality. She had a keen appreciation, too, of literary lives with the hardship of many rejections in them. These, I think, with an educational *débris* consisting of a fragment of the "Bellum Britannicum," some geometrical remains, and a few dislocated facts from the "History of England," by John Richard Green, added to a comprehensive ignorance of all the practical details of literary work, were Miss Blunt's chief qualifications at the age of seventeen for the pursuit of letters.

Naturally, our aspirant wrote poems, and stories, and articles upon the seasons of the year. The poems were lugubrious to a degree to be the work of a perfectly able-bodied young person whose appetite was a family notoriety; but perhaps this was natural too. The concluding stanza of one of them, I remember, ran—

> "Alas, for the piteous yearning,
>   For the ever-increasing pain,
> For the bitterly hopeless enduring
>   When the clouds return after the rain!"

Margery sent this one to "Harper's Monthly." Fortunately she kept a copy, since the original was probably drowned in the tears of the editorial staff. It met with a violent fate of some sort, for she never heard of it again. The stories chiefly concerned young women who wore straight skirts and girdles, and masses of dark hair, and were in doubt as to the true meaning of existence—this was after a course of a certain modern novelist— and the stories, when they sought various publications, "accompanied by a stamp," usually came back to her with a polite little printed form which read, "The editor regrets," etc. Sometimes the editor did not even regret, he embezzled the stamp, and took no notice. Whereupon Margery waxed wroth, and wrote a vigorous phillipic upon the "Rights of Authors," which didn't get published either. I don't quite know how to account for the failure of the essays on the seasons, for Margery never said anything about them that was not entirely respectful and strictly true—unless the editors thought that as there never have been more than four of them, perhaps they were exhaustively discussed in the almanacs, and that especially as we have one of them almost always with us, public interest in them had rather flagged.

Margery added a few articles embodying views of life faintly reflected from "Sartor Resartus" to her pile of humiliations, wrote some savage reviews of books she did not approve of, for her own private satisfaction, and grew cynical. She still nourished her Secret Purpose, however, nourished it upon the historic rejections of "Sketches by Boz," and a large number of "snow" apples daily—snow-white inside, rosy outside—you have nothing like them in England, and I don't know at all how

7

disappointed literary aspirants console themselves in this country.

Then something happened. Margery went to Quebec with her brother for a fortnight's summer holiday. On the way she read Mr. Howells' "Chance Acquaintance," and she made her explorations in the spirit of that delightful little novel. One of them was a *calèche*-drive to the Falls of Lorette, a few miles out of the city; and Margery was so charmed by the novelty of this, and the quaint little habitant farms and the black-eyed French-Canadian babies, and the petticoated curés and chattering old dames she saw by the way, that she sat down straightway when the *calèche* clattered madly back to her granduncle's door, and wrote it all out. Then she read it over critically, and it amused her so much that she put a title on it, sent it off as a matter of habit to an illustrated magazine, and forgot, in the rush of pleasant new experiences, all about it. I suppose it was a month after her return to the cobwebs in the attic that she received a type-written letter of acceptance, signed by the editor of the magazine, asking for sketches or photographs, which she had not got, and inclosing a check for ten dollars, which would be equal, in this puzzling currency of yours, to about two pounds. If you happen to possess a file of "Outing," an American monthly of some vogue in England, I believe, you will find Margery's sketch "On Two Wheels to Lorette," without pictures, somewhere back among the seventies.

It is a curious fact that the success of this venture of Margery's marked the demolition of her Secret Purpose. One would have expected it to be quite otherwise. But after her first whirlwind of surprise and delight was overpast, she sat down with more sense than I dare say you have given her credit for thus far to ponder the natural causes that lay behind the phenomenon of an accepted contribution. Her "Lorette," she thought, had not nearly so many of the virtues of style as this or that traveled manuscript she could lay a fond finger on, and she had done it in two hours instead of the two weeks she often devoted to a "subject." It had been an airy nothing, while many of its fore-runners had cost her elaborate agonies. Why then—and Margery's brain twisted itself into a large interrogation point. I have forgotten by what process of reasoning she arrived at the answer, but she did arrive at it, and found it so satisfactory that she wrote a deduction from it up among the cobwebs on the attic wall, where I have often seen it, and where I suppose it remains to this day. This is what she wrote; it lacked all virtues of style whatever—

"Before I say anything I must have something to say."

Her ride to Lorette, unpretending little event though it was, had been something to say, something quaint, novel, interesting of its sort. It had been a thing within her power to write about, and she had written about it gayly, with the spur of fresh impressions. She came to this conclusion with some pleasure. Then she carefully applied her new-found axiom, which so many people discover much later in life, to every one of the flat little bundles she had been saving up for the remorseful appreciation of posterity, with the result, which posterity will doubtless mourn, that they were doomed to summary extinction in the kitchen fire. In her new practical light Margery found them all to be faint echoes or cheap imitations of echoes and imitations that people older and cleverer than she had disguised with a certain show of original treatment, in this way making a hackneyed thing worth hearing over again. But Margery felt that it was not in her to give an old thought a new soul; at least not yet. "Lorette" had taught her that she must have some unworn incident, some fiber of novelty or current interest to give value to her work, or be content to be her own public. And yet, as matters stood, these things were out of her reach.

Margery thought the matter over, and came to a conclusion, which led her next day to climb three flights of stairs to the office of the editor of the local evening paper. It was a very local evening paper indeed, with only one editor and only one reporter, and the editor looked extremely busy as Margery walked in and sat down among his exchanges. Margery saw that he looked busy, so she said immediately that she had come to see if she could be of any use to him. Then she unfolded her plan, which was that she should be allowed to spend a few hours every day at his office, doing such work as he could give her, and that her reward should be the knowledge of journalistic methods she would gain by it. I don't think the editor was over-joyed to accept Margery's offer of assistance; he said he was sure he didn't know what she could do, and that she would find it very uninteresting work, and would probably tire of it in a few days; but in the end he did accept it, and asked her when she would like to begin.

"This afternoon," said Margery, taking off her gloves.

The editor rang a bell, and there presently appeared from below a small boy with a very black face, whom he instructed to give the young lady a table and chair on the next floor, a bottle of gum, a pair of scissors, paper, and ink. Then he handed Margery a fresh pile of New York papers.

"Do you know our column 'All Sorts?'" he said, "Make it up."

This was an initiation for Margery, for she had always believed the "Sentinel's" "All Sorts" column of interesting facts and amusing incidents to be directly inspired by the editor; but she went at it with enthusiasm, and as she looked eagerly through the exchanges for the items she wanted she felt the first thrill of the journalistic spirit to her fingers' ends in an instinctive appreciation of what people like to read. I think Margery knew, after she finished clipping and pasting that column, which was at least three times as long as it need have been, that she would succeed in newspaper work, though you will very properly say that one thrill was rather unreliable ground to go upon. She went home that afternoon and read the "Sentinel" all over, picked out several other columns which she thought she could manage in it, got up the characters for proof-reading, and went to bed feeling quite capable of taking the paper off the editor's hands at an hour's notice.

Margery remained a non-commissioned officer on the staff of the "Sentinel" for two months. During that time she became tolerably expert at proof-reading, wrote columns of magazine reviews which the editor usually cut down, glowing accounts of the "closing exercises" of young ladies' academies that induced each of the graduates to buy ten copies to send to her dearest friends—which the editor approved of—and was even trusted to "treat" the subject of a new post-office for Pokiton in the editorial columns. The only thing that I remember Margery saying in that article was that the post-office was required, but as that was all there was to say, and she did it very exhaustively in seven paragraphs, the editor must have been satisfied. Other matters, however, which Margery carefully got up from the "Nineteenth Century" or the "Fortnightly," such as "The Revival of Philosophic Religions in India," and "The Future of Government by the Masses," he pigeon-holed indefinitely with the remark that he thought his public more interested in the future of their own affairs.

Then Margery considered herself qualified for higher things, and there shortly afterward appeared in her favorite of the New York exchanges the following advertisement—

A Young Lady of some experience in general journalism desires a position at a moderate salary on the staff of a newspaper of good standing. Specimens of work forwarded, and highest references given.—Address, M.B., "Sentinel" Office, Pokiton.

The advertisement appeared for a week, and at the end of the week not a single newspaper of good standing, or of any standing whatever, had opened negotiations with the young lady of some general experience in journalism who desired a staff appointment. She received instead several circulars offering to place materials for "remunerative employment"—coloring photographs, I think it was—in her hands on receipt of two dollars and a half; and I think Margery would be deeply amused now at the idea of advertising for a position in journalism.

One day about this time, a bundle of colored lithographs was left on Margery's desk at the "Sentinel." They were advertisements of the New Orleans Cotton Centennial—a World's Fair that celebrated a few years ago the exportation of the first bale of cotton from the Southern States. The lithographs came just as Margery was absorbed in Cable, the American novelist whom you know in England for the wonderful tenderness with which he has revealed the old-world life of Louisiana, and found her mind very receptive of the idea which they brought. "I will go," said Margery to herself, "to the New Orleans Cotton Centennial as special correspondent."

As a preparatory step she took a morning train for the nearest large city, called upon the managing editor of the most influential paper there, showed him her sketch in "Outing," and asked him if she could send him some letters about the "Centennial." The editor looked over the article, said he liked its style, but it was rather early to make arrangements, etc., etc., and ended by making an engagement to take six letters from Margery at five dollars a letter, with the option of refusing any that he did not like. I must tell you that this point was not easily gained, and Margery had to talk very sensibly and earnestly indeed to gain it. Then she went home and told her father of the chance she had got; and her father, being a wise man, applauded very heartily, and said he would help her. In the end Margery went southward, with a pleasant party, fifty dollars in her purse, and three or four engagements, all conditioned, to write about the great exhibition.

I should like to take you to New Orleans with Margery, and to show you what she wrote about there—not the wonders of the exhibition, for they have been many times out-wondered since, but the picturesque old city dreaming over its Spanish memories, its quaint narrow stone banquettes and its gardens of orange-trees and magnolias, its soft-voiced creoles, and its long sunny December days, full of the scent of violets and wild olive; its gay mad week of Carnival too, with all the romance that lies behind a mask, and all the merriment of a little negro dancing in a paper cup. But I can only tell you that she wrote about it with great acceptance, earned her whole expenses, and came home. Shortly after one of her editors wrote to ask her to give him a weekly article on "any social topic," and Margery did so with great joy, which in some way managed to get into the articles, so that people liked them. By and by there came another letter from the editor, with a hint in it that if Margery could conveniently take up her residence in the city his paper was published in, he could promise her more regular work of a general nature. The hint developed, when Margery wrote that she was willing, into an offer of the position on the paper which Margery now holds, with certain added duties, responsibilities, and remuneration, and the desk from which she wrote me the other day that she liked newspaper work as well as ever. I must not let you think, though, that she found it pure felicity from the beginning. Her editor, for one thing, was rather an irascible and gouty person, which did not appear in his correspondence, but was perfectly evident when he found that Margery had written, and he had unwittingly published, a rather uncomfortable review of a book by one of his intimate friends. Also when Margery talked about "the great unwashed" in an editorial, and he had to be interviewed by a deputation of the Knights of Labor, and assure them that nothing personal was intended. There were things to do, too, that were not easy; the writing, for instance, of a three-column biographical sketch for next morning's paper of a certain State governor she had never heard of before the evening he inconveniently died, and the reporting of a certain grand kermesse, in which fashionable society was deeply interested, to meet the emergency of going to press several hours before it really happened.

But Margery survived all these things, and her growing experience, with certain virtues in the way she writes when she does write well, have thus far enabled the editor to survive them too. Her present work is chiefly book reviewing, in which the instinctive perception of style that once made her think she could write books herself, serves her well, and editorial writing upon literary, artistic, and social subjects. She is twenty-three now, and she has a new ambition; it is to write a political leader.

When she mentions it, the editor smiles, I believe, and says that perhaps she may—next year.

Unknown origin, found in Stirling Library, Yale University.

## The Fountain of Youth

NEW ORLEANS, Jan. 29.—"Let us go to Florida," said Ponce de Leon. As you are probably aware, Ponce had been there before, away back in 1510, but in those days Pullman sleepers were not, nor portable cameras, nor agreeable travelling companions. Under the new order of things Ponce wanted to go again. Besides, there was another reason which found an exponent in sundry streaks of gray in his flowing hair, a certain unsteadiness in his gallant stride, and a vague remoteness about ante-breakfast editorials. If you go with us to Florida, it shall appear why all these things suggested the trip to Ponce de Leon. If you don't, you will never find out, and some day, when our venerable and much apostrophized Father Time shall come to you with similar monitions, you will bewail your folly in staying at home.

In a sacred and richly girt temple, situated under the wide arch of the Government building [at the New Orleans World's Fair], in the space otherwise somewhat meagerly adorned by Florida, sits Diana of the Chautauquans [an educational society]. She is a practical divinity, and around her hang many specimens of the work of her celestial fingers. Of course, she has another name whereby her earth-born worshippers are privileged to address her conversationally, but that shall not transpire. She has black eyes with a sparkle in them, a charming complexion, a plump figure, and firm white hands that rule her willing slaves with clemency and justice. Ponce bows before her, and his rusty sword rattles in its old Spanish scabbard as he makes his stately salute. As to the rest of us, Prof. Ochre and Rose Madder, to whom he is joined in holy matrimony, Theophilus and I—well, we also worship at her shrine, and lunch there.

"Let us go to Florida!" repeated Ponce de Leon, manipulating the corked mysteries of an exhilarating fluid labelled "Roederer." We glanced at Diana over our sandwiches and basked momentarily in her approving smile.

13

"We will go to Florida," we chimed, as musically as the sandwiches would permit, "and you, Sir Ponce, shall lead us thither."

Half-past eight found us steaming out into the dark, away from the lovely old city in whose quaint and gracious hospitality we had been reveling for weeks, with our faces turned toward the Peninsula and our attention bestowed upon the defects of the French school, as illustrated by Prof. Ochre, but suddenly arose the voice of Theophilus with an inquiry anent sleepers. There was silence for answer, and over the features of the professor stole a look of awful conviction, for he had been deputed to engage sections for the party, and it was horribly evident that he had forgotten all about it. We looked at one another in hopeless consternation as he hurriedly departed to seek an Ethopian audience with the porter, and viewed his downcast appearance with righteous indignation as he returned. "There is not," he said with painful distinctness, "a single section at present unoccupied."

"Therefore," said Diana of the Chatauquans, "we shall be obliged to—"

"Sit up all night!" in agonized chorus....

In the Arctic interim which followed let me enlighten you as to our destination. At the risk of being taken for the puffer of a patent medicine, I must tell you that the spot toward which our somewhat ancient and unimpeachably gallant knight was "personally conducting" us was his own and only original "Fountain of Eternal Youth," now authentically located near Lake de Funiak, between Tallahassee and Pensacola. Three hundred and seventy-five years had nearly exhausted the vital properties of his first bath, and, as Ponce was naturally desirous of outliving the exposition, he found further ablution highly desirable. Moreover, having heard of the philanthropic enterprise that is situated there, and is to do for the South what the parent plan has done for the North, his curiosity was aroused, as was also, in the interest of the *Post*, that of your correspondent.

The night wore on, but not apace. The usual baby lifted up its voice and wept bitterly, the patent-leather of Theophilus and the top-boots of Sir Ponce reposed together upon the seat opposite, while the owners thereof lay back and snored mightily, argumentatively and in unison....Presently a gray light crept up the sky behind some low black houses, a suburb of Pensacola.... Nine miles along the shimmering waters of Pensacola Bay, an hour or two speeding through Floridian semi-tropics, and the

Southern Chautauqua stood before us in the sweet sunlight of the balmiest January morning of my experience, an architectural fact. "This is the region, this the soil, the clime," said Ponce de Leon, misquoting, and we stood in appreciative silence. A tiny silvery lake, just one mile round, sparkled before us like a forgotten sapphire; groups of pines stood upon the grassy banks and looked at it, and a pleasant little welcoming breeze blew across from the other side and tangled itself in Rose Madder's hair. A serious-browed young Socrates, who is the secretary and whose other name is Banfill, came forward with a greeting truly classical and led the way to the hotel, where we were presently served with fried chicken and pancakes....

After breakfast we slept the sleep of the just and those who have been up all night....Then Socrates with cheerful mien accompanied us in our out-of-door explorations. He showed us the amphitheatre, seating 2,000 people, the opera house—for we are to be gay and festive as well as studious and meditative at Lake de Funiak—the schools of art, cookery, music and theology....

It remained for Theophilus of New Orleans to start a bonfire as the colour faded out of the west and the lake grew eloquent with shadows. And the flames leaped and flashed among the pine knots and cones, and the sparks went whirling up into the air as the incense-laden darkness came down and the silver crescent of the new moon showed sharp and clear over Chautauqua. As we passed we looked through a boardinghouse window and saw a musical group about a little melodeon. A tall, sad-eyed, middle-aged working man, with an appeal in his homely face eloquent of grief and struggle, was singing with a strong yearning in his voice, "When Shall the Harvest Be?" Ah, the harvest will be of beautiful white sheaves, sheaves of love and faith and the growing latitude of sweet intelligence; and the reapers will be strong and manful and sympathetic and great-hearted! And the Chautauqua of the South will be for her yet another diadem shining even as the stars.

"This," said Ponce de Leon the next day, as he sniffed the pure air and drank the clear water, "is no doubt a Paradisical spot, but we are yet a good three leagues from my vitally bubbling spring. To horse!"

Did you ever ride nine miles through the pine woods on a mustang pony? No? Then you haven't exhausted life though you may be twenty-two and *blasé* exceedingly. Over the soft brown carpet, under the exquisite light green mantle that has surely

15

fallen some tropical night like snow upon the trees, stumbling, cantering, galloping, we followed our gallant knight....

A broken bridge, a tangle of undergrowth, and visible excitement on the part of Ponce de Leon. A wild and Spanish "Huzza," as he spurred his willing steed, ploughed into a thicket of magnolias and disappeared. Breathless suspense on the part of Diana, and as suddenly her chevalier emerged in dripping garments, and knelt at her feet, transformed. With a sense of the romantic situation, the rest of us pushed on to the spring. The most fairy-like scene that mortal eyes are privileged to behold! Sixty feet to the bottom, the chronicle hath it, through the clear water one can see distinctly the waving forms of grasses, pure white pebbles, and a spur that Ponce said he dropped when he was there before. The pool is the colour of chrysoprase, and forever laughingly reflects the graceful forms of the magnolias and hemlocks that bend over it. I think it is tolerably certain that Hebe always filled her cup from here upon special occasions. Diana did anyway, and Theophilus roasted many sweet potatoes, of whose nutritive qualities the gods were unaware. Diana bathed her matchless complexion before we mounted to depart.

The rest of us are going back when a decade or two shall make it advisable. Theophilus wants to give his moustache a chance, he says. All the way back in the gloaming, we sang the simple melodies that people have always been singing. We are not vocalists, but the pines listened and waved silent encores to Rose Madder's sweet contralto. Here was an old song, too; they had heard it often before:

> "'Way down upon de Swanee river,
>     Far, far away:
> Dat's where my heart is turning ever,
>     Dar's where de old folks stay."

And the notes went up among the swaying boughs and back into the silent night. Somewhere in the pine woods I suppose they are echoing yet.

Washington *Post*, February 1, 1885.

# II    The Modern Woman

## Introduction

As a woman who had achieved striking success in the work she loved to do, Sara Jeannette Duncan was a self-assured, rather than strident, feminist. She resented the obstacles men put in the way of a woman's self-expression, but she never lacked confidence that the obstacles would sooner or later be removed. Even an article like "Risks of Insurance," which documents an injustice, seems to imply that the clear victory of woman's reason over man's stupidity will be but a matter of time.

The first article reprinted in this section, "How to Talk to a Man," makes a point Miss Duncan doubtless often applied to her own life: that to earn men's respect, women must respect themselves. She frequently conducted interviews with women who had achieved ambitious goals and might act as an inspiration to others: hence the accounts of a woman doctor, nurses, university students and women journalists found in this section. All of Sara Jeannette Duncan's models of the modern woman achieve their success through individual effort, not collective action, as "Unions for Women" makes clear.

The interview with the doctor begins with an interesting autobiographical passage which reveals that Sara's girlhood friends had similar dreams of independent success, and also managed to fulfill them. In both this article, and the others just mentioned, Miss Duncan seeks to assure her readers, and herself, that success in the world and womanliness are not incompatible. The manners of her doctor friend "weren't aggressive"; nurses "come from a well brought up class of Canadian women"; Phyllis and Psyche, the University of Toronto intellectuals, boast of their skills in making bread and puddings. Very early in her *Globe* career, Sara had plaintively asked her readers: "Can't we be professional and dress for dinner?" and had darkly hinted that "loss of the least womanly grace means loss of power."

Sara Jeannette Duncan wrote about women who continued to play the traditional feminine parts, as well as about the avant-garde. The "summer girl" is praised on the surface, but one detects some condescension towards her for her frivolousness. The deeply anxious contestants for prizes at the Exhibition's ladies' work display are pitied for their fanatical dedication to an unrewarding activity. Domestic servants, on the other hand, are urged to remain loyal to their "safe comfortable life." In this context, Sara Jeannette Duncan acknowledges the desire for equality (rebelliousness in the kitchen is a "growth of the times") but her awareness of the exploitation of women by commerce and industry makes her unwilling to accept an inevitable social change.

The essays in which Sara Jeannette Duncan attempts to weigh the respective claims of the old and the new ways ("Grandmotherly Repose," and "Advantages of Being a Modern Woman"—written within a week of each other) may seem at first sight to be rather at odds. The first essay suggests that modern women may have advanced "in knowledge and sympathy," but not in the achievement of happiness; the second stresses the advantages of enlightened education, and of progress generally. But it is clear that even as she evokes the world of her grandmother and praises it as "so safe a haven," Miss Duncan realizes that she cannot and would not attempt to return to it. "Careers, if possible, and independence anyway, we must all have." The pursuit of happiness is ultimately of less concern than the pursuit of self-fulfillment.

"Mrs. Brown's Callers," published just the day after "Grandmotherly Repose," shows that at a relatively early stage, Sara Jeannette Duncan was developing her talent not only as an essayist but also as a writer of fiction. Both dim-witted society women and the single-minded Mrs. F. Suffrage are mocked; the satire, as is often the case in Miss Duncan's work, seems directed at unimaginative thinking in general, rather than at a specific social attitude. In this respect, and in its clever mimicry of society types, "Mrs. Brown's Callers" anticipates similar scenes in the novels that began to appear five years later.


## How to Talk to a Man

Walking down Sherbourne Street the other day, under the protection of my biggest umbrella, I shamelessly listened to the plaint of a sweet young creature in a lovely shade of yellow pongee, who walked directly in front of me with a fellow angel in blue.

18

"One of the cleverest men I know," said the azure damsel, "is Mr. Jones. I own to finding the youth of society rapid, as a general thing, but Mr. Jones is a brilliant exception."

"Mr. Jones" came from behind the yellow parasol. "I think him the most abandoned idiot of my acquaintance. I never see him that he doesn't remark in the most insensitive way, 'Miss Smith, what is your opinion of the effect of the moon upon Toronto Bay?' or something equally stimulating. I don't see where you find intellectuality in Mr. Jones. I couldn't with a microscope."

The pair fluttered along Gerrard Street, and I lost the blue vindication of Mr. Jones, but it occurred to me that the yellow rouge had made an unconsciously damaging admission—an admission constantly made by the sex of its wearer. "Why will men keep their frivolous moods for women?" is a cry as old as strong-mindedness. It is not always just. There are men who feel degraded and belittled by constant polite small talk or vulgar chaff in their intercourse with women, men who with instinctive gallantry bring the best at their intellectual disposal to their conversation with them. And where the accusation is merited, it is a knife that cuts both ways. One does not discuss social problems with children, but the comparative merits of toffee and sugarsticks. Nothing is more palpably and admirably characteristic of man than his anxiety to please woman, conversationally and otherwise. He brings her the flower of his sentiment and the weeds of his conversation in one bouquet, and is confident that the combination suits her. And his confidence is not without ground in experience, and has only recently been misplaced in fact.

If women desire the homage of intellect as well as of heart, if they resent eternal flippancy, and prefer to take life conversationally, as they are compelled to take it otherwise, *au serieux*, there is only one thing for it, and there is nothing startlingly original about that—they must deepen and broaden their sympathies, brighten their intellectual activities, energize themselves by occasionally bathing in the great tide of human affairs that flows resistlessly past every door-step of every home. It is useless to protest against an ignominy, and neglect to remove the cause. And above all things, girls, don't tell anybody you find a clever man stupid.

*The Globe*, July 8, 1886.

# A Woman Doctor

One June day in 1880 three girls picnicked in the jolliest way in Dundurn Park under the very shadow of Sir Allan Macnab's little old white Hamilton Castle. Burlington Bay shimmered away into the blue distance at their feet, woodpeckers tapped over their heads, tiny yellow butterflies fluttered among the gay little wild flowers in the grass, and the sunlight fell down through the wind-stirred branches upon three very earnest and enthusiastic persons indeed, as they discussed hard-boiled eggs and other things. Things present and to come; things practical and sentimental; facts and visions; "fixed fate, free will, foreknowledge absolute" to the latest thing in millinery—is there anything, I wonder, that girls will not talk about in a picnic of three with no man within a mile to listen and revile! Most of their speculations, I remember, concerned the Future and the Sex, and they pronounced both with capital letters. The speculations were wide and deep, but they had a peculiarly contracted personal application. Callow youth of the masculine order is not the only variety that possesses a wildly exhilerated opinion of itself.

I said three girls, but one had committed the indiscretion of matrimony the year before. Her fate, of course, was settled in the pessimistic opinion of the other two. The second had just received High School honours and had college ambitions; the third, who hated such things, looked affectionately upon a large and ambitious daub in oils that was secured in the fork of a sapling nearby, as in some way typical of a dazzling future career in art. Today the married girl occupies with credit a professor's chair in the Kingston Women's Medical College. She occupies another chair in different quarters with equal credit, I believe—a rocking-chair. There is one baby in Canada that will receive scientific attention from its earliest youth. The second girl is now a practicing physician in the city of Toronto with excellent prospects. The third—well, it doesn't matter about her.

I went to see number two yesterday in her unprofessional capacity. No, you shan't be told her name, at least in this column, but a very little enquiry will convince you that she is no hypothetical M.D. She came in with an aspect of professional seriousness which she dropped, however, upon recognizing me, and at my special request, did not assume again while I stayed. As she led the way into her cosy little office, I carefully observed her for evidences of that loss of womanly attributes which is so necessary a result of a medical course, but I was disappointed. She didn't stride, she wasn't a guy, she didn't use slang, her manners weren't aggressive. *Tout au contraire*. She walked well, she was dressed with taste, she talked excellently, and her manners were admirable. Most astonishing of all, when a small boy came in with a fishhook driven as far into his middle finger as the self-destructive instinct of that queer little animal can drive it, she didn't go about it in any cold-blooded or brutal manner whatever, but extracted it just as deftly and tenderly as if she had been the little fiend's mother, plus firmness and knowledge and minus hysterics.

"What do you find the chief difficulty in your practice so far?" I said, as soon as I recovered from my scientific surroundings. "Lack of confidence?"

"To a certain extent, yes," she replied. "People are very apt to be unfair to a doctor who is a woman. An incident occurred just the other day which positively enraged me. I had a severe case of inflammation of the bowels. Patient, a young girl, was doing well. Everything was going beautifully. The girl, in fact, was convalescent. The other day, contrary to my orders, she got up, went about the house, ate all sorts of stuff, and naturally enough, was taken very ill again in the night. Then her friends, instead of sending for me, concluded that things were so serious that they must have a man, and the case was handed over to somebody who has the additional distinction of trousers. That wasn't fair, was it?"

I said it was not.

"Yes," she went on, "I don't blame people for their prejudice against women doctors. They are not accountable for that. It is the effect of time, and time only can efface it. But I do think that if they employ a woman they should give her the same chance that they would a man."

"And do the patients treat you as they would a male physician?"

"They ask more questions than they would a man. They seem to think that a woman should be communicative, and they often want all the intricacies of their cases explained to them. That is a nuisance sometimes. They try to take more liberties, and occasionally I hear a maddening remark about a 'regular doctor.' But that is only among 'ignorant people.'"

"Do they all call you Doctor?"

"No; but I snub them if they don't. They stutter 'Mrs.,' and then stumble on to 'Miss,' when I quietly interpolate 'Doctor,' and after that I get my title."

44514

"Do you treat men?"

"Yes; if I am employed by the family, I treat the male members, or where I know the person, or in a case of emergency. But one is obliged to use a certain amount of discrimination about it. My speciality is, of course, diseases of women and children."

"And what about recognition by the profession?"

"I have received it on all hands. The Toronto physicians have been most courteous. I have been made to feel quite as comfortable in the medical profession as I could be in any quarter of 'woman's sphere.'"

"Well," I said, "good-bye. I'm going to put you in the paper. Tell me one thing. Have you ever been sorry you're a doctor and not something better suited to your feminine tastes and womanly predilections?"

And, will you believe it, she laughed at the idea—laughed at her feminine tastes and womanly predilections!

Here's a state of things!

*The Globe*, August 23, 1886.


## Risks of Insurance


I would be insured. Straightway I betook myself to an English accident insurance company's office to ascertain the nature of the preliminaries. It was in an unfamiliar part of the city, dingy, and populous, and given over to be the habitation of brokers. Not a petticoat was to be seen in all the length and breadth of the street. The elevator boy looked curiously at me as we ascended, the clerks stared. I felt like a book agent, but I persevered. Presently I was ushered into the inner sanctum of a tall and portly gentleman, who inquired, in a voice of patient condescension, what my business might be.

"I want to take out an accident insurance policy," I said. "May it please your gracious majesty," I wanted to add, but I didn't.

"Ah! You know, of course, the restrictions under which we issue policies to ladies?"

"No," I said. "I don't. I know of a good many restrictions under which my unfortunate sex is compelled to labour, but I haven't heard of any that apply specially to insurance policies."

"Well," responded Pooh Bah, "they unhappily exist. There is a strong prejudice against insuring women at all against accident. Our company, however, I am happy to say, has so far conquered this prejudice as to issue accident policies to such women as we consider good risks. Now you, I should think from your appearance, would be a very good risk."

"Indeed!" I said. "Thanks. I have been known as an excellent loss, but I think I would prefer being a good risk. And how much do you pay me if I get hurt?"

"That is a truly feminine interpretation," *dit* Pooh Bah, with a far away smile of superiority. "It wholly depends upon the amount of your policy what sum we pay you, and upon whether you are sufficiently hurt that we pay you anything at all."

"Really! And may I enquire how much is sufficient in your idea of accident that requires compensation?"

"Well, you see, our policies, when held by women, are only paid in the event of—of decease."

"Then I've got to die first?"

"That, unfortunately, is our rule."

"It makes a difference, doesn't it? Now my idea of a memento included some sort of compensation to myself at so much per week for the long or short but more or less unpleasant time that should precede that event, in case the conspiracy of the Toronto contractors against my connection with the sidewalk should prove fatal."

He looked at me with some anxiety, but doubtless concluded that it was only temporary.

"Am I to understand that you grant policies to men payable in the event of death and partially payable in the event of accident, but to women payable only in the event of death? And why?"

"The prejudice is an old one, and has its roots in the absolute control that husbands formerly had over their wives. A man might insure his wife's life against accident and then take pains to bring the accident about, you see. He might—as an illustration—he might throw her into the well!"

Whereupon it occured to me that we should be thankful for pumps as well as higher education.

"Further," said His Insuranceship, "it is much more difficult to define the precise extent of injury to a woman, or to know what constitutes accident in her case. A man might inflict a blow upon his wife with a domestic utensil—"

23

"Merely corroborative detail intended to give verisimilitude to an otherwise bald and uninteresting narrative." Said I absently—"He might hit her with a poker. Go on."

"—and she would doubtless consider it an accident, whereas we might look upon it in the nature of legitimate warfare."

"From a masculine point of view," I said, "it would doubtless be legitimate warfare. But proceed."

"Not—not precisely," he said, "not privately—personally—I mean—in my opinion—it's very warm today!"

"Yes," I said, "it's very warm. I believe I will bid you good afternoon."

"And you think you will not take out one of our policies. I assure you you could not do a better thing for—for the future."

"Yes," I said, "no doubt—for the future. But as a present and ever-present defence against the possibilities of the King Street pavement, your policy would be, in the language of 'Don Onofrio,' 'of no use at all.'"

If he had seen *Don Caesar* I suppose it would have been different, but as it was I heard him distinctly remark as I re-entered the elevator that they never issued policies to lunatics anyway.

*The Globe*, September 1, 1886.


## Ladies' Work at the Exhibition

I stood in the most sacred precinct of woman's sphere yesterday. I stood there a long time, for there was nothing to sit down on but some embroidered cushions, and they were under glass. This particular spot of her sphere is about the only one yet uninvaded by the usurper man. He cooks, he mends, he knits stockings, he makes dresses, he trims hats; it is little wonder that she finds it necessary to enlarge her boundaries. But this is by the way. As you will have guessed, I stood yesterday within the confines of that upper region at the Exhibition dedicated to be the shrine of "Ladies' work." Tumultuous were the emotions that surged within me as I gazed upon the loveliness ticketed before me, and reflected that it was all the product of my own sex, unassisted by any man, produced indeed in daily defiance of his ridicule and contumely. Such acres of plush, and satin, and Berlin wool!

24

"Surely," said I to the Superintendent, a pleasant but worried-looking little lady, who seemed to require about four times as many hands as nature had provided her with, "the exhibit is larger than usual this year?"

"Yes," she said, "larger than it has been for a long time. We have more stuff than we know what to do with."

"Anything new?" I inquired.

"Nothing specially new," she replied, "but a very great variety and beautiful work in all the departments."

Just then three lady exhibitors came up, each claiming the superintendent's instant and undivided attention. One of them had just discovered that she would like the location of her exhibit changed, another wanted to enter a firescreen her grandmother made, and didn't see why it should be ruled out because the old lady had been a few years dead, and all three desired to know to the hour and minute when the judges should give their decision. Every face wore an expression of the most harrowing anxiety; the woman who wanted her work hung where "the light would strike the gilt on the wall pocket," actually had tears in her voice. One is moved to compassion when one considers how completely this mass of coloured stitching represents the hope and ambition, the culture and pleasure of some women's lives, and reflects upon how vast a proportion of it must go unrewarded.

I left the much-besieged Superintendent, and attacked a lady exhibitor who was surveying her display with a kind of subdued ecstasy written all over her expressive countenance.

"That's a beautiful pincushion," I said, tentatively indicating a pink satin glory with a bow on it, that shone in the middle of the show-case.

"That! That's a satchel bag! Yes, I've been told by several that it's going to be admired. This whole collection's mine, and it would have been prettier and bigger only that we had so much company, company day in and day out, and of course I had to visit with them, and that took my time." "All yours!" and I gazed with astonishment upon the array of table scarfs and mantle drapes, tidies and wall pockets, toilet sets and knitted things, wall panels and China plaques. "And how long did it take you to make them, a year?"

"Six weeks," she responded, smiling rather exultantly at my amazement.

"What," thought I, "is higher education to this! What are all the achievements of the sex in literature, science, art, or political economy compared with this marvellous manipulation of plush and satin, and embroidery and 'arrasene,' all in six weeks! 'Vanity of vanities! all is vanity!' saith the preacher, and I am convinced that when the last woman professor vacates her chair, there will yet be found vast multitudes of her sisters engaged in the construction of fantasies in Berlin wool."

*The Globe*, September 8, 1886.

### The Summer Girl

....Another overwhelming allurement of the summer hotel is the certain prevalence of the person irreverently designated by the American journals last year as the "Summer Girl"....

If a definition of the Summer Girl should include an explanation of her origin and probable destiny, the social dictionary might be consulted in vain for complete information regarding her. Like the wind, we know not whence she comes nor whither she goes, further than that she usually arrives in a cab and departs in a Pullman car. We know that she is ubiquitous and charming, but her charms do not inspire us with any desire to add to our knowledge. Perhaps it is the indolence of the summer weather, perhaps it is the measure of her capacity to fill the capricious hour; but we are content to formulate a vague theory that she is an evolution of some spring wild flower, and that her Pullman departure early in September is only symbolic, in some sort, of her real taking-off at the hands of the withering autumn winds, and to accept her without question as a perennial gift of the gods. For the Summer Girl, while her feminine attributes are unimpeachable, is like the girl of no other season whatever. She is a diaphonous being, and the cool rustle of her muslins is a perpetual delight. She habitually wears a bunch of "Marguerites" in her belt and a far-away look in her eyes. A volume of Browning is another indispensable adjunct to her toilet, but she doesn't bore you with anything; if she has "views," and aspirations, and theories of the future life, she considerately regulates their expression by the state of the thermometer. She is not impressively intellectual, nor even remarkably original; but she is clever enough to be entertaining in hot weather, and her adaptability is delightful. Whatever your mood, she fits it like a flattering echo. If you are misanthropic on account of the mutton being underdone, she is gently cynical on various accounts, and never hints at the mutton. If you are disposed to quote Keats on a vine-hid corner of the hotel verandah, what eloquent sentiment the moon shows in her eyes! If your mood is gay and festive, how responsive her quips and cranks! True, she is apt in the use of a little lady-like slang, but who is repelled by that in a Summer Girl! Then she dances well, and she doesn't object to cigars. Oh, no! she is devoted to the odour; papa smokes incessantly at home! and she never commits a *betise* under any circumstances. In short, she knows precisely the purpose of her being, and fulfils it admirably; and this can be said of so few of us that it is no wonder that the Summer Girl is considered by many people the most beneficent provision of nature against the enervating influences of the solstice in which she appears.

*The Week*, September 16, 1886.


## The Life of a Nurse


The presentation of diplomas and medals to the newly-qualified nurses of the (Toronto) General Hospital took place, as you are probably not aware, on Wednesday evening. I think if you had been there I should have seen you, for outside of the people immediately connected with the hospital I don't believe there were fifty spectators of this interesting ceremony. You really should have gone, if it were only to get a glimpse of a life of which most of us have the vaguest sort of conception.

The scene of the presentation was not a cheerful one, however, and if you are afflicted with "nerves" of a hypersensitive character perhaps it's as well that you stayed at home. It took place in the operating room, and the slender audience sat in the raised benches usually occupied by the medical students. The long, narrow, extension-table in the middle of the room suggested all sorts of surgical horrors, and I looked at it till I wished I could chloroform my imagination. Then Theophilus would persist in discovering the terrifying uses of everything. Theophilus has less discrimination about matters upon which one would reasonably desire to be enlightened than anybody I ever saw! But there was no gruesome suggestion about the nurses. Such a sensible, practical, fresh-faced looking lot as they were! All young, but two or three veterans, for only those over twenty and under thirty-five are admitted; all healthy and strong and capable looking, and nearly all wearing an expression of happy contentment with the certainly rather arduous lot they have chosen. The hospital dress is of neat, light brown material, and the pretty high white caps are quite becoming to most of their wearers. Nearly all were plain white, but a few had an additional trimming of a band of black. Theophilus said he thought these distinguished the attendants of the fatal cases. Seraphima suggested that it was worn by the married nurses, and added that in her opinion the badge was most appropriate. I didn't ascertain which of these explanations was correct, and as they seem equally valuable, you may take your choice. Add to this costume a big white apron, collar, and cuffs, a bit of a flower, and a gay little pendant plush pin-cushion, and you have the *tout ensemble* of the hospital nurse as she appeared the other evening.

I watched a group of five with particular interest. They were all nice-looking girls; one had really a noble face, and one was a pretty little thing with pink cheeks, brown eyes, bangs, and a waist that I think ought to be sternly discountenanced by the authorities. I wondered how long her maltreated diaphragm would stand the laborious life its owner must lead for the next year or two, for she was evidently a freshman at her work. The other looked my ideal nurse; and I mentally registered her for my own especial benefit should the melancholy necessity for her services arise. A strong, firm, kindly face, full of intelligence and sympathy, and a figure well developed on sensible lines. The kind of nurse that would make illness an endurable affliction and convalesence a positive joy.

For these girls, perhaps you do not know, come from a well brought up class of Canadian women. This was not formerly the case, when the profession had little dignity and few rewards. But now that the services of trained nurses are eagerly sought for in every case of serious illness where the expense can be borne, now that many qualities and much knowledge is required, and the fair remuneration of ten and twelve dollars a week is paid for their services, the social condition of the nurses is vastly different from what it used to be, and as the importance of the profession becomes more widely recognized it may be depended upon to improve still further. There are now many accomplished young ladies among the uniformed nurses of the General Hospital, several daughters of clergymen, and one whose father is an English officer.

The importance of the profession, indeed, can hardly be overrated, both as a comparatively new bread-winning occupation for women and as an auxiliary to the services of the physicians. The medical testimony of this city is that during last winter alone numbers of lives were saved by the efficient professional nursing....And in view of the value to the community of a training school like that of Toronto, if for no other reason, it seems to me that the present very great deficiency in its equipment might be supplied by the philanthropic endeavor of this city. That is the lack of suitable sleeping and living accommodation for the nurses. At present their rooms are situated chiefly in the attic of the hospital. They must pass through the wards to get to them. In the summer the heat during the day is unbearable. The night nurses, who must sleep in the daytime, are continually harassed by the noises of the hospital.... To build them a comfortable house, adjoining the hospital, where they could sleep and sit and find some recreation and relaxation, eight or nine thousand dollars is required. Eight or nine thousand dollars from a populous and thriving city like Toronto is not much to ask; and I think in this case it is asked in a good cause. These girls leave comfortable homes and pleasant associations, to don the uniform and the responsibilities of a hospital nurse for two years. During that time they have four weeks holidays, two in each year. Their duties are the most trying that woman can undertake. The extent of them may be guessed from the fact that during the last year 2,499 patients passed through the hospital. They work from seven in the morning until seven at night, studying for examinations at the same time. During the first year they receive for their services, in addition to their tuition, six dollars a month; during the second, nine. This just about keeps them in books, underclothing, etc. Two hospital dresses are provided each year, and board and attendance if sick, are, of course, free.

This is not precisely an inviting form of existence, is it; and if it could be ameliorated in any way, don't you think it should be done?...Suppose we agitate it!

*The Globe*, October 8, 1886.

29

## Domestic Service

It is very generally stated that domestic service is growing into such disfavor in the eyes of the class from which it is drawn that the conditions attending its procurement are becoming more and more insupportable. So strong is the prejudice against it, we are told, that young women who would have gone unquestioningly into service ten years ago now prefer almost any sort of ill-paid factory work to the fancied degradation of a "place." Those whom the force of circumstances compels to submit to this "degradation" approach it in a spirit of antagonism, with the results which we hear lamented in every drawingroom of our acquaintance.

All this is undoubtedly true, and true not only of the United States and Canada, but of England, that stronghold of domestic conservatism. Testimony flows in from every beleaguered intelligence office, and from every trustful materfamilias who introduces the fruit of the intelligence office to her kitchen. For in this tree of the knowledge of good and evil, the evil, alas! predominates to a distressful and alarming extent. The most intelligent and self-respectful of the girls that are compelled to earn their own living by their hands, prefer to earn it in a shop or a factory, and the old time family treasure is as rare as the philosopher's stone.

The pass in which domestic service finds itself appears to many people as remarkable as regrettable. Nor is it easy to understand how girls can prefer the hard routine, the long hours, and the scanty remuneration of factory work to the duties of housemaid or cook. Over and over again they have been shown that household work, with its various and comparatively light character, is infinitely better for them from a health standpoint. Over and over again other obvious disadvantages of factory labor have been pointed out to them—disadvantages which they must soon learn by experience if they will not be taught without it. And yet the safe comfortable life of the valued domestic servant, with all the pleasant relations it involves, is neglected for other ways of living, more laborious and more exposed.

There is only one thing to be said in explanation of this. The average young woman who engages in manual labor has not advanced very far along the lines of modern thought. To her, her mistress sits in the drawingroom while she occupies the kitchen, simply by virtue of opportunity; and her wrath at the invidious distinction of location takes a more or less comprehensible shape in mutinous mutterings, and reckless smashings, and violent efforts to assert a somewhat exaggerated and top-loftical dignity. This feeling is a growth, and a pretty rapid growth, of the times, and mistresses should accommodate themselves to it. They have only accommodated themselves to it in so far as they have been absolutely compelled to. They have raged over Bridget's tyranny in the parlor, and weakly submitted to it in the kitchen. Yet in the very act of submission they preserve the old dictatorial attitude still. A woman is the most conservative being that breathes. For centuries she has exercised authority over her servants, and she cannot or will not see that the changed conditions of to-day demand that she should contract the scope of her authority, and alter its form. Feudalism survives in her domestic methods; she will not understand that there is an hour of her servant's day that is free from her possible exaction and surveillance; she cannot see that the young person engaged to scrub her floors, and wash her dishes is no longer a scullion to tremble at anybody's nod. It is this sense of personal tyranny, I believe, not the tyranny of circumstances, that renders service so hateful—the system under which it is necessary to ask permission to spend an evening out—a thing which no servant should be blamed for revolting at.

We need not despair, however, of the final comprehension of the democratic tendancy of the times by those who rule in our households. Indeed, unless we are to have a domestic reign of terror, anarchy, armed with a broom, and communism with a gridiron, such comprehension must come. Domestic service cannot vanish from off the face of the earth as some pessimistic prophets predict. While women must earn bread, the field of house labor will be filled, for the opportunities afforded by our manufactures must always be inadequate, and more or less precarious. But its basis must change to one more in conformity with the spirit of the age. Hours of labor must be fixed, in the kitchen as behind the counter, and the servant must be regarded more as the simple agent through which work is done, and less as a hired menial among whose chief qualifications is a forced humility of bearing before her hirer. Respect is above every law of station, and will go where it is deserved.

For the benefit of any young woman who is compelled to earn her bread by her own exertions, who lives, perhaps, in the country and thinks of coming to the city to enter a store in preference to family service, and who may read this Woman's World, here is a true statement of a true story. A young girl came a few weeks ago to Toronto from a small town on the Georgian Bay, to look for employment. She was respectable, intelligent, healthy, well favored, nineteen, and had aspirations above domestic service. She applied in vain at many shops on King and Yonge streets, and at last her application received favorable consideration in a large establishment on the latter. She had no experience, but even for the services of an inexperienced person of nineteen, one dollar per week seems a trifle inadequate, does it not? That was the amount of hers, in a large dry-goods store in which money is made. Thinking to work up to better wages she took the situation. She sold goods from eight o'clock in the morning till six at night, standing all the time. For one mistake in her cash book she was fined ten cents, for being five minutes late one wet morning, five cents more, which left her for her week's work the magnificent sum of eighty-five cents, a sum that would hardly pay for the wear and tear of shoe leather going from her friends' house to the shop. Learning that girls who had been employed in the same establishment for five years received only three dollars per week she gave up her situation; and took one as housemaid in a gentleman's family at eight dollars per month, where she wears a print dress at her work, has time for reading and sewing, a comfortable home, and stands well in the opinion of her employers. This is only one case out of scores.

*The Globe*, November 4, 1886.


**Grandmotherly Repose**


There is one thing which the women of today, with all their new accomplishments, high aims, and wide opportunities, are utterly and irretrievably losing. That is the repose of manner that our grandmothers possessed in so marked and pleasing a degree. Who does not instantly think of some gracious old lady of her acquaintance whose every movement is full of slow, unconscious dignity, who looks, and speaks, and folds her hands in her lap as if the triviality under discussion were of the greatest importance, whose face, so unworn by metaphysical lines, and algebraic crow's feet, and the vague unrest of scientific philosophy, it is a pleasure and a rest simply to look into! We will not be such old ladies, and the reason is not far to see. One's grandmother led a comparatively calm and unbroken existence. She passed her very early years learning to write a lady-like hand, and to play some half dozen "pieces" on the piano-forte, and to make her own underwear, and work patriarchs in worsted, and paint impossible horticulture in water colour. She married after a proper season of flowers and compliments and billet-doux at the age of eighteen, after which her whole existence was summed up in the prefix to her husband's name on her visiting cards. She loved that individual none the less because he was disposed to be a trifle autocratic with her, and she trusted him in everything. She knew nothing of business, and "politicks" might have been disseminated in Hebrew for all she was enlightened by the method then in vogue. Her interests hung upon the ring of her bunch of keys, were piled up in the linen closet, and bottled up in the storeroom. She had a large and promising family which she instructed in manners and the catechism and other useful accomplishments. Above all things she preserved her authority in her household; her children did not tyrannize over her. She accepted trouble and loss with resignation as part of life's discipline, and next to Providence she revered the "Royal Family." Her life was calm and satisfying, and upon the basis of knowing and doing her duty as wife, mother, and hostess this gentle ineffable repose grew with the years. But her grand-daughters begin the dead languages before they are thoroughly acquainted with their own, and attain a certain altitude in the higher mathematics before she had finished the multiplication tables. They take a supercilious glance at Kensington stitch and arrasene, and a University course. They read the newspapers and know the world, which she didn't. They are on familiar terms with various authors which, had they written in her time, she would have regarded with upraised hands and unmitigated horror. After graduation from some educational institution, the next thing is a career, a thing which, indulged in by a woman, led, in our grandmothers' opinion, sooner or later, to the gallows. I remember once entertaining, and unguardedly expressing, at the age of nine, a wild desire to write a novel.

"Put it out of your mind, my dear," nodded a placid old lady of the last century over her knitting. "Novel-making women always come to some bad end."

Careers, if possible, and independence anyway, we must all have, as musicians, artists, writers, teachers, lawyers, doctors, ministers, or something. Politics are beginning to fascinate us, and we have concluded that we want to vote. We have opinions on the European imbroglio, and we wish them treated with respect. Marriage is an incidental and seldom entered upon before twenty-two or three. There are more old maids than there used to be, and as they usually are well-employed and have no time for gossip and tea drinking, the spinster standard is becoming elevated. Modern invention has so lightened the cares of housekeeping that the modern girl asks no more special education for it than she can attain in six months before marriage, and that much time she can usually depend upon. So her whole existence, including its hopes, and aims, and occupations, is changed from that of her grandmother. Of course she has gained immeasurably in knowledge and sympathy. Her life touches universal life at far more points than her grandmother's did, and pleasure and profit may be gained from all such contact. Her accomplishment is far greater, of course, though I doubt if her sense of it is. The satisfaction afforded by one of those flowered chintz patchwork quilts, all made by hand, must have been as great as anything in the realm of feminine accomplishment to-day. She is not much happier either, though she fancies she must be; for happiness is altogether relative, and can proceed from the parchment that covered jam jars, inscribed "apricot," as well as from the piece that contains the Latin words of your diploma. After all, girls, there are worse places in the world than woman's domestic sphere, contracted though it seems to be; and while necessity and the laws of progress have driven us out of it to some extent, we can still look and sometimes go back to it with love and gratitude for so safe a haven.

*The Globe*, November 12, 1886.


## Mrs. Brown's Callers


Editor, Woman's World: I am Mrs. Brown. Not Mrs. Peter Poindexter Brown, nor Mrs. Q. Frank Antenuptial Browne, nor any of those people; but Mrs. John Brown—plain Mrs. Brown, as John is fond of saying when he wishes to turn his better half into ridicule on the score of her "pug," which used, by the way, to be a *nez retroussé* in the days before she became plain Mrs. Brown. Like most people who want to see their friends in Toronto, I have a "day" upon which I don my oldest dinner-dress, for John is on a salary and I have to be careful, and receive in my little drawingroom, which I consider quite a gem to be furnished on one hundred and fifty dollars. A good many people come to see me, if I am plain Mrs. Brown; and thinking the types might be interestingly familiar to the general public, that is, general womankind, I jotted them down last Thursday night after the last petticoat had ceased to darken my portals.

Ring number one—Mrs. Smythe-Jones. Have met her only once, and am in an agony of indecision whether to address her as "Mrs. Smythe-Jones" or plain "Mrs. Jones"! How any woman could expect to be apostrophized Smythe-Jones I cannot imagine. It's a simple outrage, in view of the contracted amount of lung power corsets have left the modern woman.... "How do you do, Mrs. m-m-m-Jones?"

Great Zeus! The very bows on her bonnet stand erect with her wrath. I do not doubt for an instant that her hair is on end within. Her response reminds me that I have not taken Greeley's Arctic book back to the Public Library yet, and that one day last week the thermometer fell to zero. I stand confounded, I stumble, I falter, I press her to be seated upon Bobby's rocking-horse, which he will drag all over the house, I cap the climax by anxiously inquiring, "And how is Mr. Smythe-Jones!!!"

This does not appease her. She evidently suspects me of ridicule, though nothing could be further from my intention; and her remarks continue to remind me of what Greeley must have suffered. She refers pointedly to a missionary society with which I am connected, and asks me if I attended the last meeting. I say I didn't, on account of the day being sore and my throat being wet or something like that, and she gives me to understand that although she was suffering severely from neuralgia she felt it her duty to go, and there were only three others present. I reflect that she might have remembered I wasn't one of them without exposing me to the humiliation of confessing it, and the bell rings again.

Mrs. Smythe-Jones departs amid my entreaties that she will come again, and I welcome Mrs. Tit-Willow whom I haven't seen for a perfect age. The dear little woman flutters in, embraces me, and poises on the extreme edge of a very big chair.

She always will sit that way, though it keeps one on the *qui vive* all the time for fear she will fall off, because if she sits farther back her feet won't touch the floor, and she says the temptation to swing them is irresistible. Then she began to chirp.

"You dear thing, how tired you do look! Really quite pale, and so hollow about the eyes, as if you hadn't slept for a week of Sundays! Now, don't tell me the baby's teething already, and you've been up with him all night! And how do you get along with Sarah! Such a temper as she has, hasn't she? I never could put up with her when she graced my kitchen, I assure you! No wonder you look worn out! It must be an everlasting combat to get anything done!"

Here I manage to interpolate that baby has all the teeth that can possibly be expected of him for some months to come, that I never was better in my life, that I find Sarah a perfect treasure, and never have a word with her.

"Really, now! Then you must be worried about something, my dear, or you've been up late waiting for John."

"Mr. Brown," I respond with dignity, "is always in the house to dinner and never—that is, seldom—leaves it again without me. That is, excepting lodge nights, when he is always—always," I repeat, with firmness, "in before eleven."

"Is it possible! How different from most men! Now, if I were making the marriage service over again, I'd put in a clause prohibiting lodge nights....Ah, here's Mrs. Cavillous. Mrs. Cavillous, I'm sure you tell your daughters every day of their lives to be old maids, if they ever expect to know true happiness, don't you?"

"No, I don't indeed, I assure you. Yes, thanks Mrs. Brown, my tea is just right. A little too much sugar, that's all"— vigorously stirring. "If marriage weren't such a lottery, I should really push the dear girls. As it is, I leave them to Providence. If everybody were only as fortunate as you, Mrs. Brown! Although it is really too bad that he should have light hair when yours is so fair. The next generation is sure to be red-haired, and it is so hard to get the colour out of the family. And I must say it's unfortunate that his grandmother died of consumption. I trembled for you when I heard him cough so the other morning in church."

"Thanks," I say chillingly, "but it wasn't necessary....John had his life insured yesterday, and the insurance people's doctor said he was perfectly sound."

Mrs. Titwillow—"Oh, how could you let him! It's so

dangerous! They always die immediately!"

Mrs. Cavillous—"I didn't like to frighten you, Mrs. Brown, but it really isn't safe to trust to those insurance people's verdict. They are playing their own game. All they want is to get him to insure and they'll flatter him into anything!"

"Oh, no!" I exclaim. "Why, they're anxious to show that he may go—go off at any time."

"All the more reason, my dear," says Mrs. Tit-Willow, "that you shouldn't allow him to have anything to do with them...."

Then comes Mrs. F. Suffrage, who wants me to take an active part in the "Cause," and desires to know if I voted in the last school elections. Finding that I didn't, she is divided between amazement at my culpable lack of interest where the Public Schools are concerned, and a throe of self commiseration at the thought that I, who might have voted, would not, and that she, who would have voted, might not. The fact is that the elections came on just in the middle of Bobby's measles, and I wonder what I employ a daily governess for, if I've got to go out and vote whether I want to or not! Then she inquires what I think of Imperial Federation, and I tell her I haven't yet given the subject the attention it deserves, having had two pink lunches and one blue one this week, and ask her when it came out....

Exeunt omnes—and enter my Belle, my well beloved, who never stays long enough. Belle tells me how well I'm looking, and admires my new water colour more than any picture in the house. She has brought me that clever new novel of Stevenson's, and a book by Marion Harland—a woman whom I adore. She disposes of every scrap of cake there is left—the dear girl—and asks me for the recipe for it. She was at the Lionwell's crush the night before, and tells me all about it. She is tremendously interested in my trouble with the seamstress over Bobby's little nightgowns, and has brought a table scarf over for me to see she worked for Nannie Hunt's wedding present, which is perfectly lovely. She brings in with her the whole fresh, pleasant, outside world. She is never bored and never self-conscious, and always the most agreeable caller on anybody's "day." Why can't people all be Belles? As I said before.

MRS. BROWN

*The Globe*, November 13, 1886.

## Advantages of Being A Modern Woman

As you are probably well aware, my sisters, to-morrow is Thanksgiving Day. It is not so very long since we imported the laudable custom of our American cousins, but quite long enough for one of its chief features to have taken such strong hold upon our affections as to make the approach of the occasion very evident to every housekeeper. Thanksgiving turkey, with all that doth accompany or flow therefrom, may be said to have become an incorporated fact in Canadian domesticity. We have not gone the length of compounding mince meat out of its due season, as the New Englanders do, nor have we taken the typical Thanksgiving pumpkin pie into our affections to any great extent as yet, but we have shown remarkable unanimity in adopting the dinner extraordinary as an indispensable feature of all true gratitude. It is both stimulative and illustrative and we have not been slow to appreciate these advantages.

So by your plenished larder, and your hot cheeks, and your floury apron, and the arrival of half a score of friends and relations, you know very well that to-morrow you will be called upon to give thanks with the rest of the people of this Dominion of Canada for all your manifold and multiplied mercies, national, social, family, civil, and religious. I have no doubt you will lump them. People always do, although the particularity with which they enumerate their tribulations is most painstaking. This department has frequently been given over to such enumeration, but will seize the present propitious occasion to make a few specifications of the other sort.

To begin at the very beginning your start in the world was made under auspices for which you would have been grateful doubtless, at the time, if you had been able to form any idea of the woes you escaped. You were not constantly jig-trotted on your nurse's knee to induce repose of mind and body. You were not swathed in uncounted yards of baby linen, which would have utterly repressed your reasonable and infantile desire to kick, and left your natural spirits no outlet but your lungs. You were not made acquainted with distilled liquor and the necessity of prohibition as a preventive of cruelty to infants, at the early age of three days. You were not fed until your small organs of deglutition and digestion utterly rebelled and your whole wretched little internal structure arose in a colicky protest. You were not put to sleep by the assistance of laudanum and Mrs. Winslow, and occasionally, when you wept for it, you were given a mouthful of water! All of which was reversed in the experience of the babies of the last generation.

Froebel hadn't influenced modern educational ideas as he did later when you were a very small girl, and there were no kindergartens. But your father and mother knew that romping and fresh air were important factors in your development, and while you may have learned your alphabet under the old system, you were not compelled to sit in the house and sew samplers and keep your petticoats clean, your slippers in shape, and your hair in curl, because you were a little girl. You climbed apple trees and fences and tore your clothes and raced and rioted and had as generally good and uproarious a time as your brothers had. Perhaps you even played hockey with them—I did, with crooked sticks and wrinkled horse-chestnuts, in intervals of taffy-making, over a big kitchen floor. And all this helped to lay the foundation for your excellent constitution which meets the wear and tear of the world's demand upon it so well to-day.

But the small creatures in pinafores of your mother's day were served not so.

When you went to school you were permitted to learn Latin if you wanted to, and to revel in the higher mathematics if you were so inclined. You had the fun of beating your cousin Tom at trigonometry, and topping the class in an examination in Greek prose. Science invited you, and you ruined three aprons, nearly deprived yourself of your right thumb, and burst twenty-seven glass tubes in learning how to make a certain acid with a most inexpressible smell. True, you couldn't make it now, even if you wanted to, and you don't remember much of your chemical research, and you couldn't analyze your own baking powder, nevertheless one Julia Jones who researched at the same time you did now occupies an excellent position in a ladies' college by virtue of the opportunity. Then you could have matriculated if you had so decided, and if it had not been for Jack no doubt you would have been to-day a graduate of a university of which he is not the president, and faculty, and Senate combined.

Which educational advantages were not known to the maidens of the last generation.

Jack was not the first who attempted to interfere with your university career by several people. But the possibility of other than domestic channels for your womanly activity made you critical and careful. So you said "No" till you couldn't help

39

"Yes," which is a course so admirable that it is here held up for emulation by every young woman whose eyes rest upon your causes for thanksgiving. You could afford to wait till Jack came or to dispense with a matrimonial prospect altogether, although Jack was an incident you rather hoped for and have never regretted.

But in the olden time the girl who refused a man who was willing and able to support her in comfort assumed a responsibility for her future that is rather alarming to think of.

And now that you and Jack are housekeeping, haven't you got a patent cradle, and an improved kitchen range, and hot and cold water, and stationary wash tubs, and a magic sewing machine silent and dexterous, and a carpet-sweeper, and a book which tells you how to furnish a house artistically with red flannel and empty flour barrels for three hundred and fifty dollars, and photogravures and Public Library books, and ten cent editions of the philosophers, and the prospect of casting an early and unbiassed vote, and the sweetest baby girl in the world who will have a great many more advantages than her mother ever had!

Yes, if you follow Old Aunt Chloe's advice and "Tink ob y'er mercies," it is very evident that your meditations will be long and not unprofitable to-morrow; and it is tolerably certain, too, that however Jack may rail at the deplorable feminine tendancies of the age, upon hearing your enumeration of them, his thankfulness will not be less than yours.

*The Globe*, November 17, 1886.


## Unions for Women

There is a gradual movement toward organization into unions among the women of New York who earn their bread by toil. Just now the necktie makers, who only receive thirty cents for making a dozen neckties, and who can make but a dozen a day, are holding meetings, preliminary to organization.—Philadelphia Press.

We hear a good deal now-a-days about this "movement" in the ranks of working women. Almost every metropolitan newspaper one picks up contains some account of meetings for organization, and almost every branch of the handicraft in which women engage seems to be represented by those who attend them. It seems a subject for congratulation, until one reflects upon the remarkable absence of any logical result of such union—any help afforded by it, any wrong righted. This reflection checks our gratulatory mood, and makes us cast about for a reason.

It may lie, of course, in the youth of the movement among women. It has taken years to bring it to a state of comparative efficiency among men. The perfecting of a systematic government of any body, especially of any laboring body, requires time above all things. Woman, moreover, being infinitely slower in adapting herself to the conditions of any law of which she is not herself the arbiter, less should be expected of her in results of controlled and organized effort than of her brother.

Having made these allowances, it is still true that if a plan to further the interests of any class is to receive the confidence of the community, it must show some progress, however small. If we cannot expect fruit in a month or a year, we may at least look for signs of life in buds and leaves.

The assimilation of the union idea among working women is in itself an evidence of a growing intelligence as to their own condition....Who would like to say how recently every working woman was to her fellow an enemy to be watched and dreaded, if not openly at least in the secret places where motive is born...It is assuredly very lately indeed that women have discerned the power in union, the value to themselves of their fellow-workers' labour, the momentum of a mass....

But in their emulation of manly methods have not these women workers forgotten that they are not men—that they are quite without the resources by which men hope to succeed when they agitate for what they believe to be their rights? The vast majority of working women are almost entirely without capital. I mean, of course, the capital of skill. They have spent no time in acquiring it, no effort in increasing the slender stock they possess. They have little or nothing, therefore, to deprive their employers of, and are thus practically unable to avail themselves of the most popular and most legitimate method in vogue among unions of workingmen. We do not hear of unions of hod-carriers or farm labourers. Yet the work women do for the most part is quite as elementary as that of the hod-carrier or the farm labourer. At every step downward in the scale of labour one finds additional multitudes clinging to its less precarious foothold, and at the bottom all hungry humanity seems to stand, by comparison with the few who have managed to climb. And so it will be but a trifling inconvenience to the employers if their women employees refuse to work at their price. A few hours, and the places will be gladly filled. And as a rule, we cannot blame the employers. If business and philanthropy attempt to walk hand in hand in the jostling thoroughfare of this world of ours, business will surely trip and both will be trampled upon.

In the trades union ideas as adopted by women there are doubtless advantages—advantages of counsel, of ability to appeal to public opinion as a body, of clearer comprehension of their own condition from seeing it reflected in the mass as well as the individual. But to make union accomplish direct benefit in the way of more pay for less work, it seems to me that the sex should begin at the conditions which make union successful. It is possible to have machinery too elaborate and expensive for the value of the product it is to work upon.

*The Globe,* January 31, 1887.


**University Women**


The editor was certainly right, Theophilus thought, in saying that the matter should be looked into seriously for the benefit of this department, and its pros. and cons. discussed in the light of such facts as inquiry should disclose. It was impossible to overrate its general importance to the public, or to disguise the fact that it bore heavily upon the especial interests of the sex. (When Theophilus says "the sex," he always means ours; he has been drilled in the value of what we used to call at school the "distinguishing" adjective.) If excessive brain-culture had already begun its insidious work upon the under-graduate constitution; if natural feminine inclinations were being diverted out of their true channels for the futile irrigation of dreary wastes of erudition (Theophilus has a weakness for metaphors); if the blooming countenance of the Canadian maiden was gradually becoming "sicklied o'er with the pale cast of thought," and her joyous and unconfined nature had begun to lose susceptibility to compliment and caramel and all the spontaneity of youth, and to commune with itself in the dead languages, he thought it was time the public should know about it. For his part, he had no desire to see the lamp of knowledge turning all the butterflies of his acquaintance into moths.

The editor thought I might apply to the President for information, or possibly to some member of the Senate; but perhaps he had better give me a letter to Phyllis, who being a Sophomore would know more than either. And so, one bright morning not long ago, I found myself in the main hall of the university inquiring for Phyllis—inquiring with some trepidation, for it was my introduction to femininity in cap and gown. Four undergraduates of the usual kind showed me the "ladies' reading room" as one man. But Phyllis was not there, nor anybody but a gentle-voiced lady doing Kensington stitch, who seemed to have charge, and who informed me that the softer Adams of this Academe were then attending a lecture in metaphysics, but would be released in the course of half-an-hour. So I waited, and while waiting discovered that there are at present twenty-four young ladies attending lectures, the great majority of whom are in their second year. Another thing, which is not generally known, I think, or it would be more generally availed of is that by paying the fee lady non-matriculants may attend any or all of the lectures for their enjoyment and advantage apart from any condition that weighs upon the soul of the duly enrolled student. The fee is twenty dollars per term if paid in advance, and non-matriculants are charged one dollar for the use of the library. The "reading room" is nicely carpeted and furnished, well lighted and heated, a bit of green on the mantel, a big Japanese fan in the fireplace and even some articles of fancy work on the walls. The luxurious surroundings take the place of papers and magazines, however, and I could find nothing to beguile the time with but Cox on the British Commonwealth.

A hurry of feet and a rush of skirts and a sound of voices.

"Melissa, with her hand upon the lock."

And among this merry troop I find Phyllis by inquiring for her by her other name. And Phyllis introduces me to Psyche, and to a dark-eyed Senior and a fair-haired Junior and a plump little "Freshie;" and I presently am whirled into the cloak-room, where I find myself seated on the stationary washstand in a state of deep amaze listening to a eulogy upon the considerate conduct of the Hon. G.W. Ross in providing a mirror that would reflect satisfactorily six undergraduate countenances at once.

What could Theophilus have been thinking of! The amount of health and brightness and activity those girls had to spare would make existence agreeable for dozens of their sisters who refrain from taking a university course because of the strain upon the constitution. Some were more sedate than others, but most of them chattered exactly like girls who never heard of the digamma and wouldn't know a binomial theorem if they saw one. I think the subject of the metaphysical lecture was something about a dog; but I am quite convinced that Psyche will wear pink and Phyllis cream-color at the conversazione to-morrow night. And it is hereby recorded for the benefit of all who fear, like Theophilus, that natural feminine inclinations are being diverted out of their true channels for the futile irrigation of dreary wastes of erudition, that Psyche and Phyllis both deliberately prinked at the aforesaid mirror before the next lecture, to which they permitted me to accompany them. It is not at all a dreadful thing to attend. To be sure the youth masculine in the back benches stamps and sings a good deal before the arrival of the lecturer, but that is, I am assured, merely a vent for its natural exuberance. It certainly gives no word or sign of hostile demonstration at the presence of the ladies, who occupy the bench immediately under the professor's nose, and take notes with the assiduity that location makes advisable. And it opens the door for them quite as politely as it would in a drawing-room.

"Young ladies," said I, as we inspected the trilobites in the museum, "is it true that your biscuits are as difficult to raise as those things, and that the strata of your pie-crust—"

My statement was cut off untimely.

"I don't boast of my German prose," said Phyllis, "but I certainly can bake bread."

"Puddings," remarked Psyche, "are my speciality. I wish I could get the Senate to recognize my really remarkable attainments in the pudding department and give me some hope of a chair!"

"And I," added Phyllis modestly, "did the whole family preserving last summer."

Yet Phyllis and Psyche both, it may be added, take no ignominious stand upon examinations, enjoy the affection of their fellow-students and the respect of their professors, keep up their work and their dignity, and find their studies widen and deepen the pleasure and the profit they find in life.

"Come up again," they said, and I mean to. The duties and

dignities of ordinary feminine circumstances sometimes grow depressing. Domestic problems assume unsolvable proportions, and practical biology, as studied with the aid of Hibernian specimens in the kitchen, presents insuperable difficulties. When this is the case, and the constant pursuit of severe trains of thought renders a little diversion and relaxation advisable I have no doubt you would find it as I did at University College.

*The Globe*, February 24, 1887.

## A Montreal Seamstress

Once a year Christianized civilization pays a handsome dividend. Should I say civilized Christianity? Perhaps; take your choice of terms, and put the emphasis wherever you see it is most consistent with the facts. Doubtless this very general investment is always paying dividends, but only at Christmas does it make an open declaration of them, published in all the newspapers, pealed in all the bells, writ fair and large in the faces of the people in the street. We are just in receipt of our share in the general distribution, and how much richer we are, not only in gifts but in grace! Not only in tobacco-jars and shaving-cases, and sets of Browning and five o'clock tea, and Cloisonne vases and embroidered handkerchiefs and perfume bottles and *sachets*, but in that beautiful intangibility which hides itself in these outward and visible tokens and which we recognize and know to be love though it come to a sybarite in the form of a porridge bowl, to a friar in a moustache cup! Let us make the most of these invaluable returns: too soon they will slip out of their golden novelty into the dingy tint of our common assets. The Satsuma dragon that sits so consummately on his tail surrounded by a halo of artistic appreciation will degenerate into one of the "things" on the drawing-room mantel-piece; the loving kindness which transported him from the Japanese shop to illuminate your un-oriental surroundings will tarnish a little with time into the semblance of a feeling which understands *quid pro quo*. Already some of the gilt is off the gingerbread, while the blue lambkins and pink elephants are reduced to shadows of their former selves.

Of all the Christmases in Montreal I think I should have

45

liked best to see the festival at No. —, St. Dominique street. Now that the final Alleluiah for the day has died away, and the last candle has burnt out, and the remaining scraps of cold goose have been ultimately disposed of, I can say so perhaps without hinting that I should like an invitation. You don't know No. —, St. Dominique street very likely. It is not on your visiting list, and I think it improbable that any mission of charity ever took you there. The tenants did not impress me as people who would be orthodox, grateful recipients of charity. I know I did not go to give anything, but to get something. I wanted information.

It was late, quite half past nine at night, the hour when patent-leather shoes and satin slippers were about beginning to slide and slip rhythmically about the floors of party-givers, and the sated guests of notable dinner-tables to reflect upon the beauties of abstinence and the dyspeptic Nemesis lurking in to-morrow. Not that the hour is not as useful for these purposes as for any other. True, neither Tiglath-pileser nor Dorothea nor I had a ball or a dinner in our mind's eye; but that something else filled it may be partly due to the fact that so far as I know none of us were invited to one. Our choice in the disposition of the time would have had a higher moral value doubtless if we had been.

It was a rather forbidding-looking two story building before which we stopped for consultation in the frosty moonlight before entering. Might there not be *picotte* lingering beneath those low eaves and behind those close-barred windows? It was an unpleasant possibility. Or diptheria, or imported rags, or anarchy, or a police conspiracy, or Canadian tobacco? The matter of precedence being waived unanimously by Dorothea and I, it was resolved that Tiglath-pileser should go and see.

He knocked, and the knock seemed to wander indeterminately around the interior and come back without accomplishing anything. Again and again, with the same result. The door yielded to slight persuasion, and we found ourselves in a dark passage in which narrow stairs climbed up against the wall to a place where a thin streak of yellow light shone under a closed door. We sent Tiglath-pileser up.

Presently, being reassured, we followed him, and in a few minutes were smiling at one another's apprehensions. For the room we sat in was perfectly clean and wholesome. A large table full of cut cloth was outspread in the middle of it; a bit of rag carpet covered part of the floor; there was a rather battered cooking stove with a little fire in it, and on a dresser in the corner stood a whole row of those wonderful fruit plates which reward the purchaser of a certain number of pounds of a certain kind of tea. A very quaint old clock ticked solemnly behind the stove, and St. Francois Xavier divided the honors with His Holiness on the wall. One little bed with a red patchwork quilt over it stood in the other corner, and one small lamp shed rather a smoky light over all.

Yes, said the young woman with sunken eyes and high cheek bones and yellowish complexion, who stuck her needle into her shabby black dress to talk to us, she made trousers. It was a good enough trade when times were brisk, she didn't complain. And especially if she could get work from the tailors. But it was pretty hard when there wasn't much doing and she had to take it from the "ready made" shops when they didn't pay so well. She seemed anxious to talk and to be agreeable and smiled the cavernous smile that deepened the wrinkles about her dark eyes, and seemed to be an epitome of all her hard life, very often. The little children who should have been under the patchwork quilt, had tools too, one a needle and the other a smoothing iron which she drew from among the red coals and rubbed clean upon a towel with the skill of a professional. They were pretty children and the girls had curly hair. Their cheeks were red too, from that steamy, stuffy atmosphere, and they soon forgot our disturbing presence in their chatter of "Noel."

Those were her sister's children, the young woman said. Dead, yes, a year ago next Good Friday. Buried by the *Union Prières*. And, was it not lucky, she had joined just a month before! Otherwise the children could have had no black, poor things. And the old man was her father, their grandfather, but he did not hear well. The grandfather wore a very ancient velvet waistcoat, his shirt sleeves and an elaborately embroidered smoking cap. He looked up from his work with great amiability, but had nothing at all to say.

Yes, they could all help a little, but if it were not for the vest making they could not get on so well. She had another sister. There! We might hear her working the machine overhead. And for the vests they were paid twenty-five cents apiece without the button holes. Getting up at five and working till about ten you could make about four vests if you were smart, but you had to be.

And the trousers?

It altogether depended. The tailors would pay fifty cents, some even sixty. But the "ready-made" men would give only seventeen to twenty cents a pair.

It was true then—here in Montreal.

And if it were at all possible the clerks at the store would find excuse to take some of that away. They would offer a price if *"bien fait,"* and always find it *"mal fait."* For instance, she had once neglected to put the stitching in the corners of the pockets and lost all; and another time the waist bands had been cut too narrow, and for this also she was fined, though it was not her fault at all.

Why did she not go out as a seamstress or servant?

"She had never learned fine sewing—it was *"bien difficile."* And as for the kitchen, what would become of the others? And she pointed to the grandfather and the little ones.

"Truly," said she, "it is enough that I cook for these."

When we came away the old man brought his bent form as nearly as he could to a right angle with the floor, and took off the smoking cap.

The next day I saw her among the shoppers at one of those phenomenally cheap places on the cheapest street in town. From the basket on her arm protruded two webbed and feathered yellow feet, and wherever she had been for a moment there remained a more or less appetizing odor of sage and onion. She moved from the five cent counter to the eight cent counter with grave deliberation, and I have no doubt that she made good bargains.

But what they were and how they were received in the low ceiled rooms where for once, all traces of the slavery of the needle were banished away and the Christmas morning streamed as happily in over the little patchwork quilt as over the eider-down coverlets of a more luxurious locality, was not mine to see. Somehow, I wish it had been.

Montreal *Star*, December 28, 1887.

**Women in Journalism**

*Dear Garth Grafton,*
*Will you be kind enough to say something in Bric-a-Brac for the benefit of its many readers among your sex, about the prospects of women in journalism? Numbers of young ladies in*

*this city as in others, at present casting about them for useful and independent means of making a livelihood, would be grateful for the hint.*

*AN ASPIRANT.*

Perhaps the prospects of women in newspaper work may be more fairly inferred from what they have already accomplished than in any other way. And I believe that from the printer's devil up and the managing editor down, there is no position in this department of human activity which they have not filled with a certain degree of efficiency. Which is not intended to lead you to believe that even a fair proportion of the great leader-writers, correspondents or newspaper directors of the world are women. This is not true and it will be long, I think, in the nature of things before it will be true. [But] it is an unquestionable fact that women are doing all kinds of work for the press, and receiving all kinds of salaries, and that while the bulk of this work is of an inferior kind, as the bulk of all newspaper work must necessarily be, much of it has reached a very creditable level; and there are not wanting instances where real power has been exercised and actual eminence been attained by the doers thereof. Of course the field that furnishes the most notable illustrations of this is the United States. Here in Canada nothing, comparatively speaking, has been accomplished by women in journalism, partly because the Canadian newspaper world is so small as to be easily occupied by some half dozen influential journals, partly because it is a very conservative world indeed, and we know what conservatism means in relation to the scope of women's work....I suppose there are now a number of women quietly writing on the Canadian press. In fact I know that several of the more influential journals employ them constantly upon temperance work and that exclusively domestic department which most newspapers find it advisable to publish. The work of Canadian women as reporters, book reviewers and editorial writers, is also beginning to count, but we cannot be said to have done anything yet to compare with the achievements of our neighbors....

New York is the place above all others for a woman with a facile pen; and the hundreds who live there very comfortably by its exercise testify that this is very generally understood. The opportunities there for descriptive work are almost unlimited, and it is in descriptive work that women accomplish most. Reporting, with its unhesitating word and rapid phrase, its necessity for vigilance and penetration and perseverance and the ability to condense is not so well suited to their rather limited and uncertain views of things and their diffusive inclinations in talking about them. But for correspondence, in which women naturally revel, the great heart of the metropolis pumping out its daily and nightly sensation supply for the whole republic, offers material without end. Special articles of a light sort are also in great demand, for the vast newspaper-devouring public that does not care one jot to be edified, but requires unceasingly to be amused. These can be written and are written readily by women. Lately, too, certain novel experiences have been undergone by very enterprising dames, to be used later as material for sensational writing: the "Nellie Bly" expedition to the mad-house, the course of training taken by somebody else who wanted to tell the world about the ballet, the adventures of another who described the treatment given her when she "dressed up" and went begging. Of course these things do not come within what is considered the legitimate scope of women's work on newspapers, and are by no means of necessity a part of any woman's experience on the press....

The "prospects" are good now, "Aspirant," and will improve as women grow more familiar with affairs and increase their ability to deal with them forcibly behind the editorial "we." The work is much better adapted for women than much else that they do. But here as elsewhere it must not be forgotten that there are difficulties in the way which look insuperable at first and can only be surmounted by the exercise of the divinest kind of patience.

Montreal *Star*, January 25, 1888.

# III    Society and Politics

## Introduction

Sara Jeannette Duncan's talent for minute social observation is evident throughout this section. Care in documenting the exact appearance of things and attention to social conventions are, of course sources of strength in her fiction.

One suspects that Miss Duncan always had a sharp eye for signs of male oafishness in a cafeteria. Her interest in politics may have developed more gradually. Just before leaving Canada in 1888, she served for a few months as a Parliamentary correspondent for both *The Week* and the Montreal *Star*, but the social atmosphere of the capital seemed to matter more to her than the important political questions then being discussed in Parliament.

"Our Latent Loyalty," written for *The Week* nearly a year before Sara Jeannette Duncan went to Ottawa, tries to grapple with that perennial Canadian issue, The Canadian Identity. Canadians, she suggests, are like Americans in customs and egalitarian instincts, yet distinctive in their loyalty to the monarchy.

The essay's conclusions are not remarkable in themselves, but it is interesting to observe that Sara Jeannette Duncan maintains a delicate balance in evaluating the weight of American and British influences. In that respect, "Our Latent Loyalty" lends itself to an autobiographical interpretation. As the child of Scottish and Irish-Protestant parents, Sara Jeannette Duncan was a loyal daughter of the Empire; nevertheless, her literary enthusiasms were for American writers, and the United States was the scene of her early journalistic successes—a friend commented that she "always talks Washington and New Orleans when she can."

By the time she began to work for the *Indian Daily News,* Sara Jeannette Duncan had certainly become convinced of the importance of politics. Most of the editorials that seem to be hers deal with foreign policy, and a few focus on Canada. Readers of "Imperial Sentiment in Canada" were treated to a brief, pro-Liberal history course, followed by a eulogy of the coming "greatness" of imperialism. The editorial would seem to over-estimate Laurier's enthusiasm for imperialism, but it does make the shrewd point that imperialism only gained in strength when it became clear that "experiments in the opposite direction at least have failed." Writing in 1896, Sara Jeannette Duncan might well see imperialism as a force whose full impact was yet to be felt.


## Cafeterias Considered


There are few more amusing and edifying spectacles upon the chief business thoroughfare than is afforded every day from twelve to two by the various lunch-rooms of that locality, especially those that are conducted upon the "lunch-counter" system—every man his own waiting maid. Personally, I object to this fetch-and-carry arrangement. The average man at mid-day is so ferocious that his equanimity is almost invariably disturbed by a shower of hot coffee in the region of his waistcoat or a bombardment of oyster patties in any region whatever; and this, owing to his frantic manner of approaching the scene of his gastronomic solace, is all too apt to occur. His lack of equanimity under this trying circumstance almost always affects one uncomfortably, to say nothing of the disagreeable necessity of duplicating one's lunch, which is, of course, concomitant. Then there is the awful possibility of receiving the same little attention from some big blundering man of the genus whose chief end at receptions is the ruin of female attire with claret-cup, and whose awkward pilgrimage from counter to table is invariably attended by disaster of some sort. And if there is one absolutely irretrievable thing it is a milk douche over the front drape of one's autumnal habiliment. And if there is one deserving subject for something lingering with boiling oil in it it is the unspeakable person who administers it.

The lunch counter has its advantages, though, like all abused institutions. Behind it are temptingly ranged all the viands its bill-of-fare advertises, and there is no dread uncertainty about the realization of one's dreams in this respect. If things are not precisely what they seem to be on the printed *carte*, one can observe the inconsistency and act accordingly. There is no long and despairing interval, moreover, between the time one sits down and the epoch in which one's prayers are granted. Hope deferred never maketh the heart so sick as under these painful circumstances, and the sugar lumps and pickles with which restaurant-keepers endeavour to pacify their waiting patrons are all unavailing as a cure. Nor are you subjected to the nameless *hauteur* of the damsel to whose condescension you owe your refection. Your lunch is not embittered by a sense of the humiliating distinctions of caste; nor is your spirit humiliated by the saddening operation of the unnecessary snub. If Hebe had received her professional training in some of the Toronto restaurants, I think Jupiter would have refreshed himself with diminished satisfaction.

So that, on the whole, the lunch counter is not without a *raison d'être*, and it is certainly entertaining. From a point of vantage at an unoccupied table, I gazed upon the scene yesterday, with a novel sense of having discovered a new characteristic in my fellow man. It wasn't new, it was as old as the species, but I had never been struck by its manifestation as I was at that hour. I mean his faculty of nutrition. One gains no adequate idea of it by observing the ordinary biped of one's acquaintance under the forms and conditions of the family table. They hamper him, to some extent, in the display of his alimentary powers. He is beset by a haunting fear, lest by the traditional standards he should be unkindly criticized— compared, perhaps, to that unconventional animal that dines in a pen. But at the lunch counter he is restricted by nothing except his capacity; and the extent of his capacity is a beautiful sight to see. It suggests to one, among other things, the intimate nature of our connection with the animal kingdom in the scheme of creation, and a very well-defined doubt of the modern theory of man's gradual approach to a celestial individual. The silent concentration and avidity, the inconceivable rapidity, with which the long black line disposes of its pie and sandwiches, brushes its moustache, and melts away, is a unique feature of the lunch counter and is, as we used to say of the Exhibition, "well worth a visit."

Let me tell you a little incident to illustrate the remarkable tactlessness of men, since we are on this subject. I sat down to a table that would hold six, and it had but one other occupant, an elderly gentleman. Presently another elderly gentleman came in and then two young ones, and then another and another—by this time, as you may imagine, I was too disconcerted to observe whether they were patriarchs or callow youths, for they all sat down at my table. But as they had every right to be there I lunched on in apparent unconcern. Presently, elderly gentleman number one looked at me with an expression of extreme benevolence and remarked:

"I suppose you didn't know of the tables reserved for ladies?"

Of course I didn't, but the idea of telling me about it at that eleventh hour, when I couldn't possibly get up with a section of a roll and half a gill of coffee and march to the other end of the room to where I belonged! Let me warn you if ever you chance to enter a "lunch counter" place to keep a sharp lookout for signs.

But wasn't that just *like* a man?

*The Globe*, October 7, 1886.

## Christmas Cards

*DEAR MADAM—Christmas is drawing near and with the thought of its approach arise visions of roast turkey, plum puddings, Christmas presents, and Christmas cards. I have no objection to any of these but the last, and I do think that the practice of sending cards to each of one's intimate friends is assuming dimensions beyond all reason. I know fellows who annually spend from $10 to $15 in cards. The ladies to whom they are sent of course say they are exquisite and thank the senders in most extravagant terms if they have an opportunity.*

*The gentlemen look upon this practice as a nuisance, and keep it up simply because they think the ladies expect them to do so. It is time we had an understanding between us, and I appeal to you as one who is not afraid to speak out your honest conviction.*

*Will you give us the opinion of the ladies on this subject, and I have no doubt that by so doing you will relieve the pockets and consciences of a number of young men.*

*BENEDICT.*

"Benedict" has voiced the opinion of the general public. Everybody will agree with him in condemning and expostulating with the present exaggerated custom of sending Christmas cards, once so moderate, pleasant, and inexpensive a way of remembering one's friends at that festive season. And Woman's

World takes pleasure both in approving his sentiments and applauding the timeliness of their utterance.

Not so very many years ago, quite within the memory of the youngest salaried youth annually ruined by the exactions of the fashion now, we had a pleasant habit of sending little pasteboard mementos with some such simple design as a rose-bud or a bunch of violets printed thereon to certain people at Christmas time. The class of our acquaintances to whom we sent them was quite distinctly defined. It did not consist of intimate friends, for intimate friends received a long, bulging Christmas letter, and felt injured if it didn't come: nor were they mere acquaintances, for these we did not consider it necessary to remember at all. They formed the small class between, and were people to whom we wanted to send a remembrance of our good-will at a season when good-will abounds, and yet were unable or unwilling to send it in epistolary form. Very appropriate were the bright-tinted little messengers for this service, and as we sent them flying north and south and east and west, with their gay suggestions of summer past and to come, we felt a gracious sense of having done a pleasant duty. For the cards, quite primitive as they appear to our luxuriously educated eyes now-a-days, were really simple, more tasteful and more appropriate than they have ever been since. At least they meant more than they do now, for their signification in these latter days has been dreadfully watered; and after all, as they say in Sunday School presentations, it is "not the intrinsic value" that we consider in accepting some gifts.

And then the manufacturers with one eye upon human vanity and the other upon the rapid spread of the custom among all classes, began to elaborate, and from ten and twenty cents, the price of a pretty card went up to twenty-five and fifty. So long as they advanced along the lines of good taste and the increased excellence was brought about by prizes for designs, while we grumbled a little at the expense there was abundant compensation for it in the real beauty of the cards. But it was soon discovered that there was not as much profit in catering to the taste that preferred art and simplicity as to that which rejoiced in artifice and elaboration. So the best cards began to be fringed, and the effect of the design was utterly spoiled by the tawdriness of the trimming. Then satin and plush and chenille were called into requisition with the result that the cards most sought for became marvels of millinery and upholstery and

55

price.

This was not the only result. It is astonishing how many of us are so feeble-minded that if we cannot give as we fancy we should, we will not give at all; and great numbers of people who used to indulge in the pleasant custom have discontinued it simply because they can't afford its extravagance. Another is the yearly tax upon limited incomes "Benedict" mentions, for the card-sending is chiefly done by young people, and young people's incomes are usually most limited. Another is that the pretty old fashion is wholly spoiled, for almost everybody who sends these elaborate mementos does it more or less grumblingly, and almost everybody who receives them experiences more or less embarrassment in doing so. The custom is further robbed of its meaning by being too promiscuously adopted. It is no longer a special remembrance, but a very general one, and the impulse that used to move us to observe it has become dulled in the formality of habit.

As to the opinion of the ladies who receive these expensive trifles, that varies, of course, with the lady. It is not in human nature, at least not in girl human nature, not to be flattered by the devotion which induces a young man to deprive himself of a variety of things in order to expend three or four dollars upon a Christmas card for her. But it usually happens that youths with extravagant tastes in any one direction have them equally well developed in others, and their gratification in any one does not often depend upon self-denial. A young lady's opinion of the common sense that would advise the purchase of a "Merry Christmas" sentiment imbedded in several roods of plush and satin at so much a square foot is more doubtful, but that also depends upon her views of life. I know most girls think regretfully of the volumes of Browning or the quantity of new music, or the bunches of roses that the sum would represent, any of which things she could accept quite as readily as a foolish plush picture book which makes her the compliments of the season and then proceeds to make a meaningless piece of demoralization of itself by catching every atom of dust in the house.

*The Globe*, November 22, 1886.

## Our Latent Loyalty

....There is no use endeavouring to disguise our complexity. Much as we might desire to assume a virtue that we are totally without, and stand forth among the nations of the earth a simple unit with a single purpose and unadulterated methods of achieving the same, candour compels us to admit the ramifications that history and geography have conspired to bring about in us; and even while we deprecate them, to acknowledge that it is the chiefest joy of our politicians—the savour of life unto our newspapers, that they exist. Frankly confessing then that we are complex, even in the fractional sense—for does not our Government exist in Ottawa by virtue of itself and two-thirds of Quebec?—and that we are disposed to revel in the fact, let us, for the benefit of our untutored neighbour, even now engaged in a vain struggle with our national problem—endeavour to explain ourselves.

While it is by no means exceptional to find an otherwise intelligent American believing that we regularly pay to England the taxes that still make tea an odious article of diet to Bostonians of high principle, and have so affected his whole nation that the brewing of it is an unknown art to this day, believing also that our Governor General rules the land with a sway as absolute as His of all the Russias, it is no more uncommon to come upon one who has a fair knowledge of our system of government and our relation to Great Britain. Such an one, knowing our practical independence in all senses, crosses the line to find it loudly voiced by the press and echoed by the people, without animus for the most part, and without blame or remonstrance from any quarter. He discovers that similar conditions have brought about the adoption of economic principles very like his own, that the body social is governed by much the same laws, that individual opportunity exists to almost the same extent as in his native republic. He finds us tacitly acknowledging that hereditary monarchy and a privileged aristocracy have been reduced by the remorseless action of the centuries to the limited functions of the surviving castles of the feudal lords, in being landmarks of history and picturesque accessories to the national life. He finds too a very general, impersonal, unimpassioned belief that the latter will outlast the former in this pleasing capacity. He sees the honour of knighthood loftily smiled at by everyone not remotely expecting it; he hears occasionally, not often, for the fact is too patent for frequent comment, how impossible would be the existence of the English social fabric in this country. If this comes to his hearing anywhere in Western Ontario it may be voiced in nasal syllables that have a dear familiarity in his ear. He sees American goods in our shops, American methods in our advertising, American slang in our newspapers, and a large number of people desirous of following Mr. Goldwin Smith and Mr. Erastus Wiman into the broad highway of Commercial Union which Mr. Butterworth is so industriously preparing for the feet of them that love not the N[ational] P[olicy]. He may well be pardoned for supposing that one great tide of political faith and social hope and religious charity pulsates from the Arctic Ocean to the Rio Grande, national in all but name. Yet he finds even the Prohibitionists still loyally toasting Her Majesty Queen Victoria in the beverage of their preference; "God Save the Queen" still lustily rendered by Canadian lungs; her birthday still the occasion of harmlessly enthusiastic gunpowder plots; the jubilee year of her reign originally celebrated by every town and village in the Dominion; and the contemptible assailant of her representative greeted with something of the warmth his mission deserved. He comes upon a little court at Ottawa whose precincts he is kindly but firmly deterred from invading uninvited, even though he be a nabob of Gotham who has considerately telegraphed his intention beforehand. He finds the little court, alien to our social system as it is, transferred from place to place with marvellous adaptability, and whole democratic communities standing on tip-toe to see Viceroyalty drive by. He sees a tumult of enthusiasm arise wherever Their Excellencies present themselves, and he goes home perplexed to know why the ordinary piece of humanity he sends to the White House every four years cannot make his pulse beat as this fragment of an effete civilization does when the band plays the National Anthem in his honour, and all the people rise to pay him homage.

These are the facts: the explanation is less easily stated. Sentiment is difficult of analysis, and the sentiment of the flag of the most difficult sort. We owe more to Britain than we are ever likely to pay; gratitude may be detected in it. We love our Queen: for the span of a long lifetime she has been to us the embodiment of all the tender virtues of a woman, all the noble graces of a queen. Thousands of her subjects in Canada were born in her kingdom; and nothing is more contagious than the

58

loyalty they colonized with. Rideau Hall is an isolated fact in our social life. It has, and can have, no translatable meaning as a centre for the very irregular circumference it should dominate. Such old-world practices as obtain there we rather rejoice to see, feeling again in their dignity the bond of connection with the most dignified of commonwealths, and in their great incongruity, assurance that they never can become indigenous. We are glad to know that Her Majesty's representative is comfortable at Ottawa, and can be made so in his own way; and for esteeming his presence there or here an honour, with the history he bids us share, the traditions he commits to our keeping, and the flag he points our love and loyalty to, we cannot think of apologizing.

*The Week*, May 26, 1887.


## A First Lady's Brown Bread


Our dear cousins the Americans are such sincere Democrats! The incidents of place and power mean so little to them; the hideous distinctions of caste are so little known in their free, equal and enlightened midst! A striking illustration of this theory is to be found in a recent issue of the New York *World*, wherein is printed, very plain and large, a facsimile of Mrs. Grover Cleveland's recipe for brown bread, in her own hand-writing. I daresay Mrs. Cleveland's way of making brown bread is quite to be depended upon. I have no doubt that the staff of life as Mrs. Cleveland prepares it in Washington is as light and crumby and crusty as the same article upon the plebian table of Mrs. Jones in Jonesville. But the intrinsic value of the information does not seem to account satisfactorily for its prominence in Joseph Pulitzer's great newspaper. Would the recipe of Mrs. Jones of Jonesville, be religiously followed by a large majority of good American housekeepers, and carefully pasted in several thousand gilt-edged scrapbooks? It is not probable, at least unless Mrs. Jones had forsaken a noble husband and a promising family to become a society actress, or had the honour of placing the art of female pugilism on a professional basis, or had walked abroad a startling illustration of some pronounced theories of dress reform, in any of which cases her attention would have been temporarily diverted from brown bread. Mrs. Cleveland's recipe is really a rather curious comment on Republican notions. In allowing it to be published she does the most democratic thing possible herself, and directly encourages precisely the opposite thing in her fellow citizens. I had almost written subjects. Democratic or undemocratic, however, it is a very bad time for Mrs. Cleveland to be scattering recipes broadcast over the great Republic which is so shortly to say whether her lord and master is to have another term or not. She probably means well, and may do good; but the dyspeptic element of the electoral population in the United States is large, and Mrs. Cleveland is altogether too young a housekeeper to tamper with it.

Montreal *Star*, December 9, 1887.


## Imperial Sentiment in Canada

Mr. (Joseph) Chamberlain, whose plain hope it is to identify his name and period of office with the practical Federation of the British Empire, will shortly receive important assistance to this end from a quarter in which he has probably not been taught to look for it—the Liberal party in Canada, which now holds the reins of power in the Dominion. Hitherto, it might almost be supposed by the casual reader of contemporary history, that a monopoly of Canadian loyalty to the mother country was held by the Conservatives of the colony. The late Sir John Macdonald was the head and front of it, and this able politician's eloquence and plausibility were such that he contrived to stand at the head of his party as the personification of impassioned devotion to England for many years....In this connection, it is surprising to note how an accustomed way of looking at things will survive much that should conduce to another point of view. Sir John Macdonald's notable "National Policy" was conceived and carried out in plain opposition to British interest as a whole, and many of its tariff provisions were directly aimed at British manufactures....

The history of the Dominion during that time offers valuable instruction to the protectionist. The high tariff National Policy was designed, of course, to nourish home manufactures; it was promptly successful in establishing them, and for a time Canada appeared to have entered upon a period of industrial deliverance. Then the new industries began to flicker out, exhausted by their own competition in a narrow market....

Already the new Canadian Premier, the Hon. Mr. Wilfred Laurier, has found occasion to announce that he and his Liberals looked with favour upon designs for Imperial Federation based on a preferential tariff for the goods of Great Britain and her colonies. This is more than his predecessors would ever have been able to say, since their very being lay in the hands of the manufacturers. Neither, indeed, but for the experiences of the last eighteen years, would any Canadian party have been able to say it; for the innovation requires all the courage that comes of the knowledge that experiments in the opposite direction at least have failed.

Neither can it be denied that in recent years, and especially during the past year, the political outlook of the Dominion has been affected by the growth of the Imperial sentiment. Twenty or twenty-five years ago, any scheme of Federation founded thereon would not have been seriously received by the Canadian people; it is utterly beyond the range of practical politics. The views of the Manchester school were then strong in England, and were accepted as the proper interpretation of colonial destiny. All this has been changed; and during the past year or two, Canadian politics has seen the final effacement of ideas which conflict with British connection. The Venezuela embroglio, the South African question, and the progress of Australian Federation, have strongly reinforced Imperial feeling, which is now sanguine of a permanent organization of the Empire on a federal basis. The weakness of the idea has hitherto been the lack of its embodiment in any definite plan; but even its opponents are compelled to admit the vigour of the sentiment behind it; nor are they disposed to belittle the essential foundation which such sentiment supplies.

Not long ago, the Canadian Liberals, in despair at the yoke of the National Policy, took for a plank in their platform commercial union with the United States. This they have for some time definitely abandoned, being convinced of the political dangers involved; but the theory was sufficiently advertised to give an entirely wrong impression of the attitude towards Great Britain of a great and powerful political party in her most progressive colony. It is, therefore, doubly gratifying that the present Secretary of State should find the first sincere welcome to his scheme for Imperial Federation offered by the Liberals of

Canada, with whose economic principles it accords, and who are proud to claim a part in the greatness it prefigures.

*Indian Daily News*, October 7, 1896.

# IV    Cities

**Introduction**

Twelve years, and a vast amount of travel, separate the first and last pieces in this section. Yet in both essays, and in most of the others, Sara Jeannette Duncan asks fundamentally the same sort of question: how is the essential character of a place revealed symbolically by apparently insignificant habits or customs? What can one deduce from a cheap sugar-bowl in New Orleans, or from the flower bouquet a Hindu offers an Englishman at Christmas-time in Calcutta?

The New Orleans article shows a remarkable maturity and tolerance for an untravelled young woman. Sara Jeannette Duncan is evidently surprised to discover women "who would rather flirt than vote," and a leisurely pace of life "singularly unaffected by the frantic rush for advantage that overturns every other consideration in the North," yet she is willing to accept what she finds. A willingness to be curious rather than censorious never deserted her in her subsequent travels.

Washington was the next city in which Miss Duncan lived. Evidently an atmosphere dominated by a cultured aristocracy was very much to her liking; though she praises the opening of Parliament as a display of the fineness of the Canadian character, it is clear from other articles she wrote about Ottawa that she regarded our capital as lacking in the proper social forms when compared to the American capital.

Toronto was, of course, much more familiar to Sara Jeannette Duncan than either New Orleans or Washington. Perhaps familiarity tended to dull her usual powers of observation; the article on Queen's Park is, surprisingly, one of a very few that seek to analyze Toronto's nature as a community. The notion that people "blazon their class in every line of their faces" and that character can be satisfactorily defined purely in class terms, is a constant motif in Sara Jeannette Duncan's work. Her review of the Queen's Park parade is a trifle condescending for modern taste, yet she does seem to take pride in the "clean, fresh...well-meaning, intelligent" appearance of the Toronto "multitude."

Though a young Toronto couple is praised for its bourgeois virtues, Sara Jeannette Duncan also rejoiced, perhaps with more genuine feeling, in the "merry-heartedness" of the gay

Montreal Winter Carnival. During her stay in Montreal, she seemed more inclined to describe, with friendly puzzlement, the customs of French-Canadians (particularly nuns and Jesuits) than to interest herself in the activities of her Protestant brethren.

The two selections about Winnipeg reveal the difference between Sara Jeannette Duncan the journalist, and Sara Jeannette Duncan the apprentice novelist. "Winnipeg: 'The Veritable West,'" written for the Montreal *Star*, is essentially a good, factual piece of reporting. For the book version, *A Social Departure*, Sara invented a sheltered and innocent English girl named Orthodocia to be her companion and foil. It seems from the *Star* article that Miss Duncan herself was surprised by the evidences of Winnipeg civilization; in *A Social Departure*, Orthodocia's exaggerated astonishment is used as a means of satirizing British condescension towards the colonies.

The description of Tokyo is basically the same in the two versions. It is a delightful practical example of Sara Jeannette Duncan's theory, expressed in an earlier review, that a travel writer should present a scene "through the glamour of a susceptibility which is a peculiar product of the author's vision."

The two articles on Calcutta show the ambivalent view Miss Duncan took of her adopted home. The British resident in India, she contended, was doomed to be narrow in his interests by reason of his limited stake in the country. Yet (and here she provides an effective statement of the conventional view Anglo-Indians had of themselves), the Briton in exile is to be admired and pitied for the courage of his self-sacrifice.


## Peculiarities of New Orleans


....The Exposition, however, is far from being the only, or the most entertaining feature of New Orleans...Of course, the people precede the place in everybody's curiosity, and the people here are very accessible. They take Northern, and especially Canadian, interest for granted, and exert themselves to gratify it in a manner most truly amiable.

They are very much in love with their city, their habits, and their opinions, and by admiring the first and assenting to the last you win their eternal regard. The men are small, slender, sallow, vivacious and—numerous. In Northern cities every other passerby is a woman. New Orleans femininity stays at home. There are whole streets in the very heart of the city upon which a lady is never seen. One may look in vain for blocks in search of a grocery or a drygoods store on such streets, discovering at last that they are devoted to purposes exclusively male. The size and number of gents' furnishing establishments form a standing evidence of masculine vanity, the frequent tobacco shops testify to the fact that everybody smokes, and the ever recurring saloon furnishes significant data for temperance advocates. The men of New Orleans are a leisurely lot. They are singularly unaffected by the frantic rush for advantage that overturns every other consideration in the North. They have time to be agreeable, to be considerate, to enjoy things. They have known the best privileges of money, and the experience has taught them to discriminate. They are good talkers, whether they have anything to say or not. A Louisiana young man never appears to better advantage than when he is discussing nothing at all with a pretty girl....

The young ladies themselves are very young. At 17, the New Orleans girl is a charmingly developed poem, in which coquetry and an excellent idea of matrimonial necessities make well balanced metre and admirable rhyme. One seldom sees a plain-looking specimen under 22. After that the creamy complexions begin to fade and wrinkle, the dark, passionate eyes lose their lustre, the delicate, patrician noses adopt a roseate hue, and the whole beautiful structure is a collapse. But in the day of her beauty and brightness, the American girl of the South is an unparalleled example of exquisite womanhood. She would rather flirt than vote, and much prefers the acquirement of the Kensington stitch to the practice of medicine. She has numberless cousins, all deeply in love with her. She usually returns the tender passion to a limited and [discriminating] degree; but doesn't take it seriously.

Indeed, nothing is taken seriously here but coffee. Coffee is a matter of grave anxiety, of profound speculation, the key to domestic felicity, the chief factor in family jars. "By their coffee ye shall know them," is the popular maxim concerning the grocers, and dismal is the fate of the man of sugar and spices if he is weighed in the balance and found wanting in the quality of his Mocha. But the cousinly affection by the fair Louisianian is by no means to be compared with her devotion to her tiny after-dinner cup of the inspiring dark-brown fluid; and she is delightfully candid in avowing it. The society girl here has no more to say than a northern belle, but she says it better. Conversationally as well as in every other way, she is graceful, arch, and in excellent taste. She is not eloquent, but her eyes are, and the quick play of light and shadow in her face, the unobtrusive action of her little hands, and the ever-changing emphasis and inflection of her soft syllabled words put a world of meaning into her most ordinary remarks. In dress, she has tendancies decidedly French. High-heeled boots, high-crowned hats and "pullbacks," hair "pompadoured," and an unlimited amount of powder form the essentials of street costume here. I have yet to meet a pretty girl who does not enhance her beauty and hasten its destruction by the assistance of the powder puff— or a married woman, or an old maid. They all do it. If you keep your face clean you are a Northerner and a barbarian.

Literary taste is high in New Orleans. On the table in your boarding-house you will find Turgenev, Hawthorne, Arnold, James, where at home you would be greeted by such celebrities as Mary Jane Holmes, Mrs. Braddon, or The Duchess. People read with enthusiasm, but do not lionize to any great extent. [George Washington] Cable is decidedly unpopular, especially since his unfortunate expression of sympathy with the Federals in "Dr. Savier"....

Family life is an interesting revelation to Northerners. It is an odd combination of the luxuries of the past and the necessities of the present. The coffee-urn is an elegant piece of family silver, the sugar-bowl is of yesterday and cost 20 cents. Your hostess wears one silk dress and her grandmother's diamonds. There is much table ceremony over the odd Southern dishes. Gumbo, rice—infinite rice—"noodles," "daube," fried plantains, and "sheep's head"—a delicious fish—are some of the edibles to which your Northern palate accustoms itself with a readiness that the broad, benignant lady at the end of the table finds delightfully complimentary....There is something organically wrong with a vegetarian here, and to ask for cracked wheat porridge is to subject yourself to the gravest suspicion....

Christmas Eve was an experience never to be forgotten by the thousands of strangers in the city this week. About 10 o'clock Theophilus, Theophila and I took a car for Canal street. Away up in the "garden district" of the city, a mile and a half from the centre of attraction, sounds of revelry were loud and low, as the wind carried them. Once among the shops, however, the scene beggared description. Electric lights before every door showed a wild, exhilarated crowd of men, women and boys surging here, there and everywhere. The shops blazed with light and colour, the theatres were packed to the doors, and every enthusiastic Louisianian who wasn't drunk did his best to look as if he was. A tin horn was melodiously breathed into by every boy of 10, youth of 20 and grandsire of 60 who tramped festively up and down the flashing length and breadth of Canal, Common, St. Charles and Carondelet streets. Fire-crackers, cannon-crackers and torpedos made the mule's life a burden to him, as they exploded immediately under his industrious legs, and number-less rockets streamed up among the stars. The noise was like a battle. Our particular mule became so agitated that he actually jumped out of his traces and put his melancholy countenance in at the car window, to the great discomposure of Theophila, who was looking out. A deafening blast from somewhere sounded frequently and discomposingly under one's feet, at one's side, overhead, and with horrible uncertainty to the rear.

At last we reached the foot of Canal street and stood upon the broad levee. An original idea of boating upon Christmas eve seized Theophilus, and we embarked upon the ferry for Algiers, a disconsolate suburb of New Orleans across the river. The Mississippi rolled along in its broad majesty....the St. Louis packet slowing swinging out into the river sent out a broad shaft of light that made a glorious path over the murky water and transformed the dirty village on the other side into a dream of quaint architecture; and all along the further shore lay the dazzling crescent of the Queen of the South. I regret to state that Theophila took cold, and so did I. But not even the prospect of unlimited influenza could induce us to regret our experimental knowledge of a New Orleans Christmas Eve.

London (Ont.) *Advertiser*, January 6, 1885.


## Society at the American Capital


....While it would be extremely difficult to draw an actual line between the official and the unofficial resident of Washington, in favour of the latter, it may safely be said that the most potent and exclusive element of society here exists entirely apart from the office-holding class. It is a very common error to suppose that usage is dictated to the capital by the mistress of the

White House, in newspaper parlance the "first lady of the land." Nominally Mrs. Cleveland will lead society here, practically she will be led by the comparatively small, insignificant, and unostentatious fraction of society aforesaid. It is almost wholly Southern, and chiefly Virginian. It is entirely a leisure class, comprised of men and women whose culture is the product of several generations of extreme civilization, not too rich, but above the struggle for office and its attendant humiliations, not at all ambitious, but quietly tenacious of the social privileges that have always been theirs. Senators may come and go, administrations may wax and wane, but the conservative few, in their old-fashioned houses, continue to govern themselves and their capital by their own traditions, unmoved by anything but a gentle, sometimes scornful curiosity. There are always, of course, some official families who enjoy to the full all the privileges of both circles, as the Bayards and the Whitneys, but speaking generally they may be said to be concentric, revolving about the White House, one within the other, and the office-holders are on the outside. Even the social head of the democracy is necessarily democratic, but the social principle is essentially aristocratic everywhere. There are drawingrooms in Washington, therefore, strange as it may appear to people uneducated to accept the social ultimatum of a Court, from the inner sanctities of which some of the women best known in connection with the Administration find themselves debarred.

"You have men to rule you," said an American cynic to a British cynic, "who would not invite you to their tables."

"And you have men to rule you," responded the transatlantic caviller, "whom you would not invite to yours!"

A very brief sojourn in the American seat of government is sufficient to convince one of the retaliatory force of this rejoinder, and to impress one very strongly with its qualifications. It is quite an invaluable lesson, a Washington winter, in the present development of a great people, even from a social point of view. It is the only cosmopolitan city in America—the local character of New York is more marked than that of Kalamazoo. Here, from California to Maine, elected on a thousand issues, throng the fair representatives of all classes, with their families, their tricks of dialect, their ways of living, their social ideals, and the whole result of such education as varying circumstances have given them. From the hard-headed Senator Blank, from beyond the Mississippi, who occupies two chairs in his wife's drawingroom, habitually elaborates his remarks with a toothpick, and assassinates the President's American every time he makes one, to the courtly and witty Ingalls, the elected of Kansas, but the product of Massachusetts, who combines, in his barbed personality, scintillating French qualities with icy New England ones—there is an *embarras de richesse* for the sociologist.

The social privileges of Washington are probably the most accessible in the world. The visiting code in vogue is responsible for this. Everybody calls at the White House, first calls are paid by the Congressmen's wives upon the Senators' and all ladies with husbands of higher official rank. The wives of the Senators call upon those of the Chief Justices, and the *corps diplomatique.* First calls are paid, however, rather oddly, by the "ladies of the Cabinet" upon those of the Senate. As the whole round world is privileged to call upon the reception days of office-holders' wives, which calls are promptly returned and usually in person, there is practically no bar to at least the incipient stages of social intercourse in Washington. This has, with its obvious drawbacks, one grand good result in a society in which it is at least possible that every member may stand upon his or her merits. "Where else," says one of the brightest of Washington's many bright women to me the other day, "could I, single, plain, and comparatively poor, without family advantages, find the best drawingrooms of the city open to me, simply by virtue of such brains as it has pleased a compensating Providence to bestow upon me?" Truly nowhere....

If you come to Washington expecting to find a people of high average culture, of independent opinions, of wide hospitality, of a strong literary and scientific bent, of quick appreciation, and of that charming but indescribable character that is the result of the friction of widely differing personalities with the common basis of a high order of intelligence...your expectations will be abundantly realised.

*The Week*, August 12, 1886.

## Sunday Afternoon at Queen's Park

Did you ever, my estimable friend, after listening to the irreproachable discourse of your own orthodox and beloved pastor, deny yourself your Sunday afternoon nap, and betake yourself to that democratic temple whose roof is the breezy branches of the trees of Queen's Park? I assure you, whether or not you receive a spiritual benefit, your knowledge of human nature will be greatly augmented, and your city-fed lungs most refreshingly expanded by such an excursion, and it is not at all probable that your aristocratic sensibilities will be very seriously injured either.

Thither, inspired by an idle but unmischevious curiosity, strolled Theophilus and I one hot Sunday not long ago. There is not a maiden in the Queen City who does not know Theophilus. He is almost everybody's brother, and his cousinship is a marvel in the family records. He is a true Toronto type, and may be duplicated fifty times on King Street between the hours of four and six. A muscular youth, complexion various; occupation, medicine, law or banking in embryo, yachting, cricketing, lawn tennis in the last stage of development; chief characteristics, energy, usefulness, a small light cane, a pleated morning suit, and confidence in his own opinions, which is not always misplaced. There's no doubt about your acquaintance with Theophilus, you know several of him. Without further introduction then, you may accompany us to Queen's Park on any Sunday of last month that you choose to mention.

Up the long, shady, sparrow-haunted University Avenue with how motley a crowd of fellow pedestrians! And how recognizable they are! How they blazon their class in every line of their faces, in every detail of their dress! This young fellow with the swagger, and the cigar, and the air of gentility, and the brown and yellow checked suit, is an otherwise worthy member of the Order of Bucephalus, and I don't doubt figured as Master of Ceremonies in the very swell ball that Jay Gould gave last February. He seems to have occult designs upon a group of three light-hearted damsels immediately in front of him, each with a bouquet of "Marguerites" elaborately fastened to her corsage, all with tight-fitting bodices,and striped skirts very *bouffant* behind. The locks of these maidens are banged to the limit, their wrists are bangled beyond it, their grammar is bad to the farthest verge. And I think they are carrying refreshments. One has frequent occasion to meet these young ladies. On weekdays, they form a useful and efficient body of Torontonians. On Sundays, they—enhance the beauty of the landscape. This is callow youth, care-free, innocent of all but cigars and caramels and slang. In the group ahead of us there is something more. The youth with the checked trousers—he probably calls them "pants"—has inveigled one of the pink-faced young people into matrimony, and now they stroll under the oaks and maples with a perambulator adjunct. He has discarded his cigar and acquired a subdued expression. She has left off her bangles and the rose in her cheeks has faded a little. But in the perambulator which he is pushing is a little lumpy white heap, which she is forever darting forward to cover a little closer lest any wind of heaven with the thermometer at ninety should visit its precious pink contents too roughly, while he with his ruder paternity keeps a careful eye upon the stones in the road. How incomparably more to be considered is this pair and a fraction than the flamboyant couples we pass at every turn! Quite as common perhaps, quite as ungrammatical, but invested with that gentle, subtle spirit of domesticity that transmutes the basest medal of humanity into something very like fine gold.

All about us groups are standing, walking, sitting or gathered about the open-air preachers, of whom there must be at least half a dozen. Family carriages roll past, but the place is the people's, and the people come on foot. The few benches are crammed, and the grass is covered with reposeful hundreds. It is a multitude that is eminently creditable to any city, a clean, fresh, brisk, well-clad multitude, workers all of them, honest, well-meaning, intelligent people, who have arrayed themselves in their Sunday clothes and come out here to breathe God's air uncontaminated by man's factories, to see each other and to hear the preaching. Here a Cobourg graduate has gathered unto himself a large and constantly accumulating crowd. He knows the people, and he is letting them sing a verse, a little exhortation upon the verse, and then, brethren, "we'll sing the verse." And sing it they do, not with wonderful accord, but with wonderful zest. And who will say that the untrained chorus that goes up through the leaves and the branches straight through the blue empyrean to the throne of God is any less worthy to swell the volume of His everlasting praise than the Alleluias of the most expensive cathedral choir!

Here is a member of the Salvation Army engaged in impassioned discourse, contrary to received tradition and the bachelor mandate of St. Paul. Her face is pale with excitement, her ugly poke bonnet pushed back, her hands moving in untrained, ungraceful gestures as she battles with an imaginary spiritual foe to the welfare of mankind. Her audience consists largely of men, some of them of the variety of mankind from whom might be expected the most flagrant disrespect. But there is no chaff, there is decent order, and even some show of serious interest. The girl has this one infallible source of power over her wayside congregation: she believes implicitly what she is telling it. We cannot all be Dinah Morrises, or housekeepers, or partners in the german at the Yacht Club ball. If some of us elect to wear Salvation Army clothes and renounce the circus and preach the gospel to the halt and the blind in Queen's Park, I don't see that the rest of us who go to divine worship in the tailor-made suits and listen to the cultured interpretations of the Holy Scriptures have any reason to protest.

At least that's what I told Theophilus on our way home. And Theophilus switched the seed-balls off the dandelions with his bamboo stick and said he didn't know about that. He didn't understand the precise connection between a tailor-made suit and theology, and a Salvation Army suit and mobology. But you and I know that the Theophiluses of this degenerate age never do understand these things, and congratulate ourselves, I dare say, that it is not necessary that they should.

*The Globe*, July 13, 1886.


## Montreal Winter Carnival

What a blessed escape the snowshoe and the toboggan, with their decrees in the matter of wardrobe afford unhappy man, condemned the year round to garments of sober cut and dreary color—black and brown and ashen grey, with the trifling variation afforded by linen in summer and corduroy in winter! How he must rejoice in his gay knickerbockers and his streaming sash, and his tuque with the flaunting tassel, and all the rest of his carnival "togs"! I am moved to these reflections by the ardor and persistency with which the Montreal young man dons and walks abroad in his. Many-colored and ubiquitous, you encounter him everywhere and at all hours dragging a toboggan to the top of the Jacques Cartier slide, devoting his hearty Canadian appetite to the consumption of oysters in the Windsor *cafe*, giving a blanket-covered arm and a tender glance to a maiden in corresponding array under one of those lamp-posts that reveal so much more to the general public than the municipal authorities require of them. And truly, gallant gentlemen, the garb is most becoming, and sets off a well-turned knee and ankle, a broad shoulder and a shapely head as well as anything that could possibly be devised for the purpose. Of course, while it enhances good looks, it also emphasises what our Yankee friends call "homeliness," but that is true of any extraordinary garment whatever.

You will never have a complete and accurate idea of youthful Canada till you see the wonderful arch that it makes of itself for the benefit of Their Excellencies, who drive under it in the carnival procession, and hear the lusty cheers it sends up in their honor. Such an impression it gives you of youth and health, and vigor, and merry-heartedness you certainly can't get anywhere else. The arch yesterday was the largest and most elaborate yet erected, and was quite a marvel of picturesque color and posing. The prettiest costume worn by the clubs composing it was universally conceded to be the St. George. It is white, with pale blue stripes, navy blue tuque and scarf.

The procession was an event in itself, to fix the carnival in one's memory for an indefinite period. Prancing chargers came first, of course, and their riders, being of the Montreal Cavalry, looked somewhat less uncomfortable than the ordinary citizen when he mounts a curvetting steed and attempts to lead a procession. Then came a magnificent six-in-hand driven by Mr. Hugh Paton, then Lord and Lady Lansdowne, Captain Streatfield and a small Fitzmaurice, four-in-hand, then more outsiders, and then the long uproarious line of horn-blowing revelers with all sorts of vehicles, from the tiny low wooden sled of the *habitant*, to the immense pyramidal floats of the snow-shoe clubs. Handsome sleighs with splendid horses, driven by iron-whiskered gentlemen who suggested financial security, and containing luxurious, fur-clad dames who suggested financial insecurity, gave dignity to the procession which stood vastly in need of it. Such shouting and singing, and costuming; such blaring of tin trumpets; and beating of gongs; such whimsical speeches and false faces; such shouts of recognition and betrayal; such wild, general, infectious, uncontrollable hilarity!

As the last of the carnival-keepers disappeared over Beaver Hall hill, we concluded to inspect the "Lumberman's Camp" on Phillips square. We found that altogether too many people had concluded likewise, and the throng that pressed about the low log building in the middle of the square was something that you must have been jostled by to form any adequate impression of.

*"Prenez garde!"* shouted the tall policeman. *"Tenez donc!"* but it made no difference, the crowd strove and struggled and wedged itself in, and many were the bonnets that were offered up at the sacrificially low door that admitted us to the dark and odorous interior. A huge fire snapped and blazed in the middle and the smoke rose up through the roof, all of it that could not find accommodation in the various corners of the building, which was not much, to be sure. The hut was constructed, of course, of pine logs, and the interstices filled up with moss, as everybody knows they are in the primeval forests. Flapjacks, honored of tradition, were served to visitors for an insignificant consideration, and pork and beans *a la black strap* were also to be had by those who hungered for the dish. We did not. It was impossible to hunger for anything in that atmosphere, except fresh air; and the cooking was too primitive to be appetising.

In the evening festivities centred in Victoria skating rink, where the presence of the Governor-General and party enabled the managers to charge a dollar a head admission and another dollar for a front seat in the gallery. Long before the vice-regal party arrived no more tickets could be sold for lack of room; and the large building was packed from one end to the other, when the dressing room doors were thrown open and the skaters, headed by Lord and Lady Lansdowne, took possession of the ice. Lady Lansdowne, as Anne Boleyn, looked particularly pretty in black velvet costume with pearls and white veil. She has a slender, graceful figure and a very attractive, sweet and gentle face. One would suppose her a very domestic little lady and most devoted to the temporal welfare of His Excellency the Governor-General. Lord Lansdowne was dressed as a nobleman of the seventeenth century, all in black, with hat and feather, short cape, doublet and hose, buckled shoes, and a very magnificent necklace of gold and jewels. It was an extremely becoming costume to His Excellency, whose moustache was waxed to such an alarming extent that he looked quite like the arch-villain in the play. Lady Florence Streatfield, Lady Lansdowne's niece, looked very charming as a Bohemian peasant woman, and her brother, the Hon. H. Anson, wore the most elaborate costume of the party, that of a Spanish cavalier. It was composed entirely of cream satin, embroidered with pearls. The Governor's party opened proceedings in a quadrille, in which they danced as if their terpsichorean experience had been chiefly gained on skates. Both in the quadrille and in the pretty May pole dance the skating of the visitors was very graceful.

As to the rest, and there were a great many, nearly everybody skated well, and the costumes must have quite exhausted the wardrobe of old Time, from which they were principally drawn. A celestial angel, all in white, with a pair of real feather wings, sailed around with a most mundane enjoyment of the band and the flattering stare of the multitude. His Satanic Majesty, in striking and tight fitting yellow habiliments, flashed past in pursuit of her, and when next we saw them they were skating together in perfect amity. The "queen of night" was there of course and the queen of morning, and all the other queens, ancient and modern. There were Spanish ladies in great variety, and gentlemen of every century, and pages, and ghosts and Eastern, Western, Northern and Southern belles of every clime. Whole "Mikado" troupes were there and tribe after tribe of painted, feathered, tomahawked Indians, of whom General Middleton was chief.

*The Globe*, February 15, 1887.


### Ottawa: The Opening of Parliament


Another "opening" has taken its place in the blue books of the Parliamentary Library, in the memories of those who witnessed the scene for the first time, and in the long line of similar pageants which some day will lend colour and picturesqueness to Canada's past. Our present Governor-General has performed for the last time the duty of representing his Sovereign and ours in her relation to her colonists of half a continent, and the colonists have sat decorously in rows and watched the ceremony, not without some sense of its meaning as well as of the unusual grandeur of their raiment, and the extraordinary humour of the genuflections of the Black Rod. It is doubtful indeed whether national circumstances ever before combined to bring the significance of the Speech from the Throne so strongly and sharply to the minds of those who heard it. Commercial Union, Imperial Federation, Annexation, Independence, however we would ballot for Canada's future, we cannot be deaf to the voices in the East and the voices in the West crying aloud in the hearing of ever-increasing multitudes that a change must come.

And when it does come we know that a good deal must go, amongst it certain quaint old forms that have grown dear to us perhaps. And so, in the reflected light of nineteenth-century legislative procedure, as it is in our neighbours' capital for instance, where the legislators come to order, like so many school-boys, at the tap of the Speaker's ferule and the calling of the roll, and where the cuspadore testifies all day long to at least one blessing put within general reach by a democratic form of government, every act of stately deference acquires a new importance and every knee-buckle shines with an individually valuable lustre.

It is a scene well worth a journey to witness, not only for its dignity and importance in itself as illustrating Canadian comprehension of the fitness of things, and as symbolic of our relation to the greatness of earthly Powers, but for the lesser reasons of its brilliancy as a picture, its delightful *rococo* suggestion in the matter of costumes, its materialization, for a fleeting moment, of the impressions that are fading, for most of us, between the pages of the school histories. It is something to see that unwieldy brass "bauble," the mace, borne in by the sergeant-at-arm's deputy and laid upon its cushions on the table in the midst of the gowned clerks, and to reflect upon all that has been done and undone by its authority in debates which still echo round the world. This mace of ours, by the way, is said upon Mr. Bourinot's authority to be the same used in the old Legislative Council of Canada, it having been saved from the general destruction of 1849 by one Botterel; so it is worthy of our most respectful consideration on its own account as well as on its antecedents'. Nor is it wholly unprofitable to gaze upon that functionary, the Black Rod, in the exercise of his voluntary vertebral humiliation, remembering the portentiousness of his office in other days, and the long historical succession of his bows.

Before the Governor-General, as he takes the Speech from the hand of his *aide-de-camp*, and lifts his plumed hat in acknowledgment of the dignity of the "Honourable Gentlemen of the Senate," lies a very creditable representation of the Canadian social structure. The Premier and his Ministers, the Major-General of Militia, and a few distinguished visitors representing official eminence from one or more of the Provinces, are grouped about him. At the foot of the throne-chair sit the judges of the Supreme Court on our modern adaptation of the woolsack, in their scarlet robes and capes and ermine hoods. The Senators occupy the inside row of seats, behind them their wives, daughters or lady friends in all their bravest apparel. Coming as they do from all parts of the Dominion these ladies, among whom are included the members' wives, makes an interestingly typical assemblage, and one which few Canadians would fail to point to with pride and satisfaction. The seats at the lower end of the Senate Chamber are filled with the clergy and notable visitors, where the tightly-buttoned frockcoat of the western evangelist brushes the rich purple vestments of Monseigneur. Behind the bar throng the Commons, and through the crowd may be seen the acutely intelligent faces of many of the cleverest men on the Canadian press. Over it all there is a superb surface play of colour and glitter; but the most casual observer detects under this the principal elements of a social composite which is as reasonable in theory, as abounding in opportunity, and as honourably put together as any in the world. His Excellency, in contemplating the assemblage called forth by the "opening of the House," finds in the answering regard a strong expression of national individuality.

*The Week*, March 1, 1888.


**Ottawa's Social System**


Ottawa's social system is not usually very well understood in the other cities of the Dominion. Strangers who come here are invariably puzzled by its apparent inconsistencies; and if they have not the help of some experienced steersman, or more reliable still, steerswoman, in navigating the whirl of sessional gayeties, their little individual shallops are sure to come to grief. Their ideas of the Ottawa institution are conflicting. Some people come to the Capital expecting to find society clustering about a Court; others believing they will see the official usages of a dignified democracy prevailing. What they do discover, and perhaps experience, is a mixture, in no small degree an anomalous mixture, of both. We have a democratic Government with an aristocratic head. The noble pair who represent our Sovereign for us find no native aristocracy with which to form a social circle in which they could mingle freely. One natural result is that social intercourse at Rideau Hall is mainly along certain undeviating lines dictated by the requirements of vice-regal hospitality, and another that the general social body falls back from the divinity that doth hedge a lord, upon its own devices of form and ceremony.

It goes without saying that Rideau Hall is the omnipotent force in the society of the Capital, although it does operate so remotely, itself so little affected by its operation. Recognition from Rideau is absolutely necessary to any measure of success. To the outward eye, such recognition is easily obtained, the process consisting apparently of a quarter of an hour's drive to Government House, the inscribing of the aspirant's name upon the visiting books in the presence of a red-jacketed orderly, and the drive back again. This, as a rule, is followed by a card from Her Excellency for the first large affair at Government House, but by no means always, the list being carefully gone over to ensure the invitation of such people only as are included in the elastic terms "lady" and "gentleman." Somewhat smaller is the list of those whom Lady Lansdowne honours with invitations to her Saturday afternoon "At Homes," when Their Excellencies join their guests in skating and tobogganing from three to six. Most exclusive among the entertainments that have at all a general character are the musical and theatrical parties, which are not usually given, I believe, during the session, when Their Excellencies' hospitality consists chiefly of a succession of official dinner-parties. Guests are bidden to these at half-past seven, and usually depart pretty promptly at ten, a very few minutes being spent in the drawing-room after dinner. Occasionally, the crust of officialism is broken through by somebody as sure of approval in breaking it as His Excellency's brother-in-law, and the entertainment assumes a more informal character, but this happens but rarely. Dinner-parties at Rideau, in so far as resident Ottawa society is concerned, are usually very formally and strictly regulated. Official position rules. Young ladies, unless they are at the head of their fathers' households, are not asked, nor are widows as a rule, or other irresponsible and disconnected individuals, whatever their social position in Ottawa, who are without the claim constituted by a husband's official position. And during the season, I understand, it is the rule to entertain at dinner the Cabinet Ministers, Senators, members and their wives to the temporary exclusion of Ottawa people not directly concerned in the business of legislating.

Nobody dreams of questioning the fact that Rideau rules;

and very few people are discontented with its sway, which was never more than now large-hearted, adaptive, agreeable, and in its details of hospitality all that the gracious sway of Her Majesty's representative could be. Its rule is supreme, but unrelated in a manner. The official world obeys this higher law in the direction of its path, but turns very comfortably on its own axis all the while....

Montreal *Star*, March 12, 1888.

## Winnipeg: "The Veritable West"

One's feeling about Winnipeg, just rolling over its splendid streets in a cab and before speaking to a soul in it, is a vague perception of breadth and calm and promise. The city seems lying in a dream, content for the moment with having shown her magnificent possibilities; yet there is a certainty in her very repose that some day, and sooner perhaps than even the optimists think, she will arise and fulfill them. You gain at once, too, the thoroughly satisfactory impression that this is the veritable West, which is borne out in all that you see of business and society. There is no compromise with the East, no imitations, no mixing of meretricious old things and crude new ones. Winnipeg is honestly and openly new, in people, in brick and mortar, in ways and manners. It is very tonic.

Another thing that one does not expect in Winnipeg, for some inexplicable reason, is the artistic modern wooden house. Why Eastlake and the reign of Queen Anne should be shut out of one's western conceptions does not readily appear, perhaps because the shanty of the pioneer is so intimately associated with prairie architecture, but they are shut out; and chairs of "antique oak," tiled fire places and Kaga vases, strike one oddly for a while. Yet the "Fort Rouge district" is full of such houses, each with its gables, its square windows, its modern dress of neutral paint, each set in a wilderness of oak and poplar, and each with its pleasant glimpse of the brown Assiniboine rolling past. Tennis lawns there are and boat houses on the rear grounds that slope down to the water's edge. Past them six canoes abreast, full of young men and maidens, singing as they float down the river in the clear moonlight of the prairies, often

79

make an idyllic picture on a summer evening. In this district, on the river bank, stands the famous monument to the boom built by Mr. A.W. Ross, but never quite finished or wholly occupied by anybody. It is a magnificent deep red brick mansion, ornamented in terra cotta, and rises among the autumn color of the tangle of trees about it with a pathetic harmony. Every imported brick in it is popularly said to have cost ten cents, the whole expense to have reached seventy-five thousand dollars. Nobody in Winnipeg can afford to buy it, nobody cares to rent it in its present state at seventy dollars a month. So there it stands with the September sun shining on it, a few central rooms sheltering a family or two, the rest as the carpenters left them— one of fortune's splendid bubbles which she turned into the semblance of a home and then cruelly left uninhabitable. Across the river from here one can see Government House and the quarters of the Mounted Infantry School. Down on the bank a couple of buglers are practising a call. Their red coats make a color focus for the whole broad scene, their bugle notes slip pleasantly down the river on the quiet air. It might be a call to the East—a call of faith and hope and courage for the time that is to be.

As Government House is undergoing repairs and has been almost ever since Lieut.-Governor and Mrs. Schultz entered it, it is impossible to get a very definite idea of the character of the new *regime*. By opening the Legislature in citizen's dress His Honor has given one indication that it is to be marked by a disregard for the forms and ceremonies of the past, a departure which is variously commented upon. On the other hand, dinner-going society in Winnipeg will welcome the change from the "cold water" repasts of the late administration.

Society in Winnipeg is noticeably young, with the high-spiritedness of youth and something of its impatience of control. Its friendliness, without restraint or reserve, is delightful. We found relations of such amity existing that the unexpected friends of a temporary bachelor might be taken to breakfast at an absent neighbor's—truly a test of fraternity. There appears to be a great abundance of young men in the place, young Englishmen, and English-Canadians. The number to be met at a five o'clock tea, usually contemned of masculinity, is surprising. Femininity is chiefly youthful, pretty and married. Something in the air of the country makes everybody vivacious—whether the extraordinary attractiveness of the young married ladies is to be accounted for on general grounds by the climate or not, is difficult to say....

The wail of domestic Winnipeg is for servants. A car-load or two of the semi-experienced cooks and housemaids who are earning from six to eight dollars a month in the smaller cities of Ontario and Quebec could find ready employment here at from twelve to fifteen dollars. Two applicants only resulted lately from an advertisement of a week's standing for a general servant, at fifteen dollars, for "family of two." One was an Icelander, who spoke no English and could not cook, the other an English school teacher with higher certificates, who had abandoned the educational for the culinary field. The inter-provincial "carrying trade" in neat-handed Phyllises might be stimulated to advantage.

In real estate bargains occur every day. A few shrewd quiet people, who either kept out of the boom or arrived after it was spent are laying the foundation of very pretty fortunes which a few years must realize. The Federal Bank sold the other day to a young lawyer from Ontario the most beautiful building sites for private houses in Winnipeg, twenty lots for six thousand dollars. The frontage varies, but the average price was three hundred dollars for a fair-sized lot, sloping down to the run behind, in the best wooded part of Winnipeg, and in what divides with Fort Rouge the advantage of being the city's fashionable quarter—Armstrong's Point. The lots run straight from the fine old Bannantine Mansion to the Water Works, and must be a familiar bit of land to all who know anything of real estate transactions in boom times....

As you know, the boom swept away old Fort Garry. It would have been worth yearly thousands to future Winnipeg as a bit of pioneer history of the most fascinating sort, but the thick-headed controllers of the city's destiny at that time could see nothing but the immediate realization of its value in dollars and cents. It went into the hands of the Philistines and now nothing is left but a few bare lots on Main street, with the old gate to the fort and Government House of the Hudson Bay autocrats still standing solidly against the advances of shops and hotels. It is about the most astounding piece of utterly ignorant, stupid and vulgar administration that Canada affords, especially when one thinks that it was done not in Winnipeg's early history but within a decade of to-day.

Montreal *Star*, October 6, 1888.

## Winnipeg and Orthodocia

I don't think the emigration agents have left much to say seriously about Winnipeg, which they probably call the "Prairie City," and chromo-lithograph in other ways with their usual skill, so I will treat it from Orthodocia's point of view, which cannot be called serious. Her first surprise was a cab—a four-wheeler, with two horses. Her next was the popular style of architecture. "Queen Anne!" she said under her breath. "I distinctly understood that the settlers lived in log huts!"

....Our Winnipeg hostess lived in one of the Queen Anne houses, and I could perceive Orthodocia's astonishment rising within her as she observed the ordinary interior garnishings of Turkish rugs and Japanese vases and Spode teacups. "I rather expected," she said to me privately, "deers' horns and things." And when I sarcastically suggested wampum and war hatchets, she answered with humble sincerity, "Yes." Orthodocia's wonder culminated at an afternoon "At home" at Government House, where, as the local paper put it next day, "the wealth and fashion" of Winnipeg gathered together to drink claret-cup and amuse itself. There were the Governor and his A.D.C.'s, there was a Bishop, there were the matrimonial adjuncts of the Governor and the Bishop, equally impressive; there was a Canadian Knight and his dame, there were judges and barristers, and officers and visiting celebrities, and a rumour of a real lord in one end of what the local paper called the "spacious apartments." I was rather glad Orthodocia didn't find any Indian chiefs there, as she expected, though perhaps she would have preferred that sensation; and I was distinctly gratified when I passed her in conversation with a younger son in corduroys at the reception, looking glum, who had just come out to waste his substance in Manitoba, and heard him inform her that "Weally, you know, for natives—it's weally wathah wum."

The reason he found it "wathah wum," was because he had a shooting-jacket on and people were looking at him. They all wear corduroys at first—to dances and the opera indiscriminately, by way of helping the "natives" to feel on an equality with them. But in the course of time they commonly go back to the usages of civilization.

*A Social Departure* (1890).

# A House in Tokyo

I am afraid you must allow me the present tense again for our housekeeping in Japan. To live a week in Tokyo is to forget entirely how one got there, and to write about it is to disbelieve that one has ever come away. The great purple stretches of the prairies are blurred like a badly-washed water-colour in my recollection now, our gallant mounted policemen are uniformed in flowing *kimonos* with hieroglyphics on their backs, the Blackfeet carry on fan flirtations, the Rockies form a dissolving chain of Fusi-Yamas, and even the Great Glacier, as I try to think about it, folds itself up and retires behind a lacquered screen in my imagination. There may be such a continent as America, where the inhabitants build for themselves hideous constructions of red brick and stone, sit down in them on four stiff legs instead of two flexible ones, and have never learned to put a flower in a vase—one may even have spent some part of a previous existence there, but one is quite willing to accept proofs to the contrary. There is a possibility of reality too in your big London with its shuffling multitudes. But there is nothing certain any more in the world except these pale half-lights that fall on the blackened tiles of the curving roofs of Tokyo, creeping up to the faint yellow sky of a November evening, nothing but the swaying drops of light that begin to reel across the moats, where the dark water under the arched bridges catches and holds them undissolved for a fleet moment, nothing but a queer white castle in a gnarled tangle of fantastic pine trees, a pair of illogical liquid brown eyes, a great grey stone image seated silent in a silent grove....

Our house has a wooden fence around it which reaches to the second storey. There is a swinging gate in the fence, which will admit us if we take our hats off. From the outside our habitation cannot be described as attractive. It is much too retiring. Within the fence the house proper disappears again behind a sort of shuttered shell, which is closed up at night, making our domicile blankly unresponsive to the public eye....

Come inside. The vestibule, you see, is about the size of a packing-box; we are careful never to turn round in it. A pair of ladder-like little stairs go straight up in front of you. The slide to the right leads to the kitchen—ah, the kitchen!—the slide to the left into the drawing-room. This apartment is neatly furnished with a picture. The picture represents a hermit in a severe spasm, blowing a little imp out of him. Orthodocia says that in the same room with that hermit you really do not feel the need of ordinary drawing-room garnishings. He is so tremendously effective. But I would like another picture showing him in a state of convalescence. Part of the walls are plastered and part of heavy paper panels. The plastered part runs two feet and a half round the room at the top and all the way down on one side, and is coloured a soft dull brown. The panels reach from the plaster to the floor, and are in delicate shades of biscuit-colour, decorated in silver....The floor is covered with thick, soft yellowish straw mats, bound with blue cloth and joined together so as to make an artistic design, and the windows are simply panels, divided into little panes and covered with the thinnest, most porous white paper. A very pleasant subdued light comes through them. The window panels slide in grooves like the others, and the whole house is intercommunicative; that is to say, if Orthodocia stands in the vestibule and strikes a match, I can tell in the seclusion of our remotest apartment on the next flat whether it lights or not. If you come upstairs you must wait until I get to the top to be out of danger of my heels. The steps are smooth and polished, and very pretty to look at, no doubt, but it is a littly trying to be obliged to take off one's slippers every morning and throw them to the bottom to avoid descending *à la* toboggan. Our two small bedrooms are slightly less ornate repetitions of the *salon* below, only that the sliding panels in various places disclose cupboards. In one you see, neatly rolled away, the Japanese quilted *futons* of our nightly repose, in another the requisites of the toilet, in another a wardrobe...We do not yet know our resources in cupboards, or the precise walls to take down to go into any special apartment, and are constantly discovering new ones by getting into them by mistake. Yes, we have our domestic difficulties—no household however humble is without them—but those you must hear another time. Shall I try to be polite to you in Japanese?

Be good enough to favour our poor domicile by taking a mat. Doubtless your honourable feet are tired. This tea is worthless indeed and green, yet deign to moisten your gracious lips with it, and make the cup an heirloom in the family....

You must be going? Ah, is it not well not to speak so? There is nothing under our humble roof that could possibly please you, yet is it not well to wait a little?...*Sayonara!* then—*sayonara!*

*A Social Departure* (1890).

## Public Spirit in Calcutta

If the intelligent globe-trotter, who is already beginning to disembark along the Strand, tarried long enough among us, he would infallibly be struck by one essential difference between the Briton in India and the Briton at home—the almost total absence of anything like a vital interest in the local public affairs of this country. We do not seek to imply that there is any lack of "shop" in general conversation; it might indeed be freely admitted that dinner tables suffer from rather too much of it.... But more careful scrutiny reveals that immediate personal interest that so universally explains the button-holer's discourse—he is the promoter of the railway or the shareholder in the mine, he has made up his departmental mind that the road-cess should be differently adjusted, or that the Mahomedan law of inheritance should be amended, or that Government House should be provided with a bicycle stand for use of His Excellency's advisers on Council days. The individual ever carries the personal interest to exhausting lengths, and his listener is often reduced to the profane conviction that it does not matter one earthly trifle what happens in the particular connection under discussion. But let him turn the conversation upon any point where the benefit of the one is merged in that of the many, and he will find, as a rule, both ignorance and apathy....

The colonial takes root in his New Zealand, in his Canada. He acquires permanent interests, unknown to our shifting community, whose sole contingency of permanence lies in Circular Road [the cemetary]. The men of permanent interests must consider ultimate effects, the transient money-maker of ten or twenty years can afford to ignore them. It is a common saying that Anglo-India is indifferent, so long as nothing is done that threatens immediate personal interests or rouses race antagonisms....

That this indifference is seriously to be deplored few will deny. It renders the task of those who would further the general benefit infinitely harder by playing directly into the hands of the active few whose interests are invariably found to suffer in any change proposed for the good of the community at large....

*Indian Daily News*, December 11, 1896.

# A Calcutta Christmas

Once again, Christmas Day has come to remind us how permanent are the institutions of the Briton even in exile and under conditions as far as possible removed from those of his native land. In every one of his Eastern footholds today the *naif* marigold garland testifies that the non-participating Oriental is nevertheless respectful and well-wishing, and in India in particular, Europeans are perhaps a little overwhelmed with the cloying trifles that mark native sympathy. In the absence, however, of almost all that is significant of the day at home, we might well hesitate to dispense with the bazaar bouquet, the "dali" of sweetmeats and similar inevitables which have come to be part of it in India. The frosty chime is not in the church-bells, nor the accustomed flavour in the plum-pudding. More than all, the children are not here, and Christmas is pre-eminently a children's festival. Perhaps the excellent digestion of other days is absent, too, and few indeed are the fortunate families that can gather in anything like an unbroken circle about whatever does duty for the Christmas hearth. Nevertheless, the day brings its own spirit, and unites old associations to enforce it. Admitting its local drawbacks, we must, nevertheless, rejoice, in all that it means, and if it has meant more in other years, in the anticipation that it may mean more again. A Merry Christmas, therefore, to all our readers—the merriest possible.

*Indian Daily News*, December 25, 1896.

# V  Institutions

## Introduction

While she worked for *The Globe*, Sara Jeannette Duncan wrote an extensive series of articles on benevolent institutions: a home for newsboys, a home for destitute girls, a night school for working-class men and other such charities. Any modern reader who has come to take the welfare state for granted will find in these columns startling evidence of the extremely limited resources private charities had at their disposal in Sara Jeannette Duncan's time.

Miss Duncan herself could hardly be expected to anticipate the transformation in social thinking the 20th century was to bring. In the *Globe* articles (particularly "The House of Industry"), she frequently reflects the conventional attitudes of her time: the wretches sinful and extravagant enough to need charity had better be grateful for it.

Sara Jeannette Duncan wrote fewer articles of this type when she moved on to the Montreal *Star*. "Women's Medical College," with its defence of professional, but not social or political, daring, is similar in spirit to many of the articles in the section on the Modern Woman. "Notre Dame Hospital" is somewhat less characteristic. Miss Duncan seems to have believed in theory that the contemplation of suffering induces compassion and humility (this principle is stated in the opening paragraphs of both "Toronto Sick Children's Hospital" and "Notre Dame Hospital"), but usually she manages in practice to keep her emotional distance from the victims of life. But in "Notre Dame Hospital," and "A Montreal Seamstress," written two days earlier, she seems startled into a genuine emotional awareness of the pain inflicted by illness and poverty.

Readers of Sara Jeannette Duncan's novel, *The Path of a Star*, will know that she was no friend of the Salvation Army. The novel contains an account of a Salvation Army meeting, with many of the same details as in the newspaper report given here, but in the fictional version Miss Duncan allows herself to be more sharply satiric.

## Toronto Sick Children's Hospital

As most people are aware, the Sick Children's Hospital is now situated upon Jarvis st., near Adelaide, in the building that used to be the Notre Dame. If you find your heart growing harder with comfort and health and happiness, as hearts will under such circumstances, I would advise you to take note of its location, and the fact that you may be admitted very afternoon from two to four. The good you may do the hospital will really be insignificant beside the good the hospital may do you.

Miss Cody, a graduate of the Toronto General Hospital, is superintendent of this one, and as we chatted in her pleasant little parlor I asked her about the life the nurses lead during their two years of training.

"Is it not very laborious?" I inquired.

"Of course it is not easy work," said Miss Cody, with a smile. "We are prepared for that when we enter. The position is one of great responsibility, and its duties are fatiguing, especially at night. But it is very satisfying work. One feels that she is accomplishing something in helping to relieve suffering and doing what she can to restore health"....

I learned from Miss Cody that the Sick Children's Hospital is supported mainly by public donations, although it receives a Government grant of fifteen cents a day per capita, which amounted in 1885 to $1,473, and a city grant of $600. There is no canvassing, no solicitation for the Hospital. The ladies who manage it trust entirely to Providence for all necessary funds, and thus far they have not been disappointed....

"It is quite wonderful," said Miss Cody, "how strong a hold this charity has taken on public sympathy. Never a week passes during which we do not receive donations of fruit or flowers or clothing for the children...."

"And how many have you in the Hospital at present?"

"There are thirty-three under treatment. Some half dozen are well enough to be out of bed, but the majority are prisoners in their little cots."

"Do you find any special disease predominating?"

"By far the majority of the children are afflicted with hip-joint disease. Sometimes we cure and always we relieve it, but as a rule the children are not brought to us until the trouble has reached a stage beyond hope of a perfect cure. Then the poor little creatures just spend the remainder of their lives here, as happy as we can make them"....

"I suppose there is a regular rate of admission?"

"Yes, the charge is $2.50 a week, and we insist, so far as possible, upon payment of something. But no child is denied admittance because of its parents' inability to pay. There is one private ward, for which the charge is $5, but that has not yet been occupied by a full-paying patient."

"No doubt you find great differences in the character of the children according to the class from which they come," I said, as I followed Miss Cody into the girls' ward of the hospital.

"Great differences," she answered. "Some of the little ones are the children of parents in reduced circumstances, but the majority come from an undeserving class. Still, some lovely children come from the veriest slums; it is marvellous that such parents could have such children."

I thought of the slime out of which the water lily grows, and Miss Cody went on.

"Most of them have been here so long that we have grown very fond of them, and we are able to find something loveable in all."

*The Globe*, November 6, 1886.


**The House of Industry**


No, it was not a cheerful place, I decided as I walked along Elm street past the high wooden fence of the House of Industry, pushed open the big gate, and rang the bell inside the vestibule. Not a cheerful place. Through the glass of the inside door one can see the wide, bare hall within, the walls scrupulously white-washed, and the floor scrupulously clean, and directly opposite the entrance a walnut panel with the names of the institution's chief benefactors emblazoned thereon, and the various amounts of their benefactions specified opposite. There is no glimpse of warmth or color anywhere; no flowers in the windows, no pictures on the walls, no mottoes over the doors, nothing but a big, well-built, well-managed illustration of charity's sterner side. That is one's impression until Mr. North opens the door. Mr. North somehow changes it. Whether it is the pleasantly shrewd features of the worthy superintendent or his kindly welcome, this chronicler deponeth not; but as a matter of fact, when Mr. North opens the door of this institution and genially remarks that, "Yes, this is the House of Industry, or some might call it, the House of Indolence, since none of its inmates work very hard," one is immediately assured that sympathy is part of its "relief," that the poetry of philanthropy is here as well as its prose.

Mr. North led the way to the Board-room, which really looks somewhat more official and business-like than such apartments when they are sacred to Boards over which the presiding genius is feminine. There is a safe in it, for instance, and oilcloth-covered tables strewn with documents of divers sorts, and a great deal of literature of the ledger-book variety. By this I would not insinuate that the lady board-rooms I have known, are adorned with bows of ribbon, and etched photographs, and antimacassars, for that would be most untrue. In fact, the nearest approach to anything that might be termed a feminine foible that I have ever observed in such a locality, was a hand-painted, blue satin pin-cushion, which served the most useful end of accommodating the various spiders and things that secured the ladies' bonnet strings when they unfastened them to talk. The insect creation having since gone out of fashion for bonnet strings, however, I have no doubt, that the pin-cushion has outgrown its usefulness as an adjunct to deliberative assemblies.

While Mr. North attended to the wants of one or two of his more clamorous pensioners, I inspected the first report of the House of Industry, which framed and hung upon the wall, forms one of the few ornaments of this uncompromising apartment. It is dated July 10, 1837, its balance is stated in pounds, shillings, and pence, the various classes of inmates it alludes to as "which," and on its weekly committee are the well remembered names of W.W. Baldwin, Alexander Stewart, and John Powell.

Then Mr. North came back, and informed me that the strictly industrial significance of the House of Industry had evaporated some time ago. The character of the institution has changed several times. It was originally a place where service for the public was performed in various ways, and paid for, as the old report testified by the City Chamberlain. Then it became a Magdalen Asylum, then an Infants' Home, and both the Boys' and Girls' Homes had their beginnings here. It is at present a permanent home for the aged, infirm, homeless, and friendless of both sexes, and a temporary one for the convalescent of the hospital without other resource, who are well enough to leave that refuge but not well enough to work for another.

"Is any age stipulated by the rules affecting inmates," I enquired.

"They come at almost any age from the hospital, but our regular inmates are all over sixty," said Mr. North, "and all are for some reason unable to support themselves. Some are blind, some have wooden limbs, some are paralyzed—all are wrecks."

"And what," said I, "is your standard of admission as regards character?"

Mr. North smiled and shook his head.

"It wouldn't do for that to be very high, ma'am," said he, "or we should have nobody to admit. Some of these poor creatures have seen better days, and are respectable enough, but after all simple ill-luck seldom brings them to this pass. For the most part, we can only say that we're sheltering here wretched remnants of misspent lives. A good many of them have seen the inside of the gaol, and would see it again if they were where temptation could find them."

"You don't boast much then of the moral tone of your establishment?"

"That's not possible in a place of this kind. But we find a great change for the better in the people who come here after they have lived in regular habits and warm shelter and on good, wholesome food for two or three weeks. They come trembling and tottering and hardly able to hold their heads up sometimes, but soon they begin to straighten up and by the time a month's passed they don't know themselves."

Then Mr. North showed me the admirable ticket system by which relief is distributed to the out-door poor, and the plan of the city by which each district is placed under the charge of a resident visitor who reports cases of want and destitution that occur in it to the board, with which excellent system the public is tolerably familiar. I was struck with the names that appeared in the various districts—they were nearly all names of such busy men! Verily to him that hath shall be given in more matters than gain alone!

In an outer room on the ground floor two or three poor people were receiving their daily dole. One pretty child, with long, brown curling hair, who carried a basket for her loaves of bread, hungrily broke the steaming crust before she turned to depart with it. Ah, poverty! how dare we whose larders are full and whose wardrobes are plenished, plead any knowledge of thee!

I saw in the store-room, which looked like a department of a wholesale grocery, packages of sugar and tea and oatmeal, which are only distributed where there is sickness. Coal and bread are the only things given away upon authorized application where there is none.

Then we went through the bare, clean, warm dormitories, the brick walls guiltless of anything but whitewash; the dispensary, where twice a week Dr. Ogden prescribes for all who come; the kitchen, where an old man with one leg and an old woman with the goitre were getting ready the savory soup-dinner of their cronies; the casual ward, where nightly now a hundred homeless wanderers find shelter and sleep, and all the other departments of this large and useful institution. In the sewing-room, mending the blue checked aprons that have come to be a badge of charity, sat a withered dame of eighty-eight.

"Eighty-eight come the twenty-fifty of May, ma'am," said she. "But I doubt if I'll see it; I doubt if I'll see it."

"Nonsense, woman," said Mr. North. "You'll outlast us all."

"I'll not that, sir. Ye mustn't judge a book by the cover, sir. Inside it may be worth jest naething, and that's the way with me, I'm thinking. But I'm eighty-eight come May, an' I've been fifty-seven years in this country, ma'am. I came out on a three years' engagement with a gentleman's family, ma'am; an' it took us eleven weeks an' three days, an' there were three clergymen aboard, an' says I to one o' them one day, says I, ma'am:— 'Do ye think we've got a Jonas aboard?' An' he said he hoped it wasn't him ma'am, an' I've been that mortified ever since!"

Another old woman, with a wooden leg, walks all the way to Bloor street every Sunday morning to church, and teaches a Sunday School there. "No weather can keep her," said Mr. North. "Rain or shine she must be off."

Then we went into the room where the men were sitting, helpless some, old and infirm every one. Two were playing a silent game of checkers in a corner, of which three or four more were interested spectators; one, an intelligent looking old Norwegian, was deep in a delapidated copy of Shakespeare, another read the familiar, magenta-covered Family Herald; but most of them sat with idle hands and chins sunk upon their breasts, their wrinkled hands clasped above their shrunken knees, their eyes fixed on vacancy. We hope it is vacancy, and not pictures of the past—an irredeemable past which holds more pain than pleasure for such as these. And we may believe it is, for under certain conditions old lenses get strangely out of focus.

For such as these what joy in the present, what hope in the future, what happiness in the time that is gone! The joy and the hope of the world surges around them and past them and they gaze at it unintelligently, having forgotten its meaning perhaps. Yet Christ was born, and lived, and died, for such as these—and the day after to-morrow is Christmas Day.

*The Globe*, December 24, 1886.

## Notre Dame Hospital

Will you try to imagine what it must be to be thankful, thankful with that dumb anguish of self-pity that brings tears to the eyes of bearded men, for an unusually good dinner! It will take a great effort to get yourself into this relation with the bountiful, well-disposed world you are born in, the world that has given you good dinners diurnally and much merriment to help digestion withal for so many years. And it will not be made so successfully as it would have been had you gone with me yesterday to the Christmas festivity at Notre Dame Hospital. There it would have been assisted by one of those rare glimpses of well-to-do humanity—and all humanity is comparatively well-to-do that can afford to spend a cent for an evening newspaper—of the dolor and the dreariness, and the lagging feet and the low horizon of humanity that is not well-to-do in its world of constant labor and of frequent pain. And this glimpse, by troubling in your soul the half-stagnant waters of compassion might have wrought more healing for you than you knew.

But you were not there, and I shall have to tell you about it. Very few people were, excepting His Grace the Archbishop and three or four Fathers, the President and a few Governors and their wives, the lady patrons of the institution and the medical men connected with it. The day was not a propitious one for hospital visiting, and I dare say a good many people are still in the torpor following their own Christmas dinners. Perhaps, too, the visitors were privileged or invited. On this point I was not informed.

93

The smell of roast turkey and the sound of gay voices met us at the very door of that queer, old, rambling, stoutly built structure, which a noble thought and some active philanthropy transformed from a worldly house of entertainment to Notre Dame Hospital. The Good Samaritan sent the bruised wayfarer to a house of refuge and paid his bill. The better Samaritan of to-day builds one for him, and there dresses his wounds, and nurses him, and prays for him, and sends him forth, if it may be, whole and rejoicing—regardless of his "denomination." I distinctly hear some excellent Presbyterian growling, "What of that!" Nothing, my friend—*rien du tout*—let us go in.

You know the hospital interior doubtless, very well. The long lines of beds on both sides of the large scrupulously clean room, with the white faces on the pillows, some gathering the hope and hue of convalescence, others drawn with suffering, others sunk in the lethargy of a struggle abandoned. Add to this familiar scene the table in the middle, bright with fruit and flowers and laden with all good things devised of the house-keepers of Montreal, and the trim figures of the patronesses. Their faces flushed with the active beneficence of carrying cranberry sauce and the rest to the bedridden ones, and most becomingly set off by the stiff white caps of the well known red cross costume. Going quietly out and in among them, mild-eyed and observant, were the best-loved of the nuns of Montreal— the sisters in gray. The visitors from the outer world mingling in gayer garb with the cassocked fathers went from bedside to bedside with subdued curiosity. As I told you, more than one poor creature cried at the sight of the grapes and oranges, and the kindness and interest and pity. And the imaged Christ looked down upon it all, not, I think, without benediction.

Nearly all the patients seemed to enjoy their Christmas dinner, but the faces of two or three turned dumbly away from it with eyes closed as if they longed to close in the unlifted oblivion which is so much better than some kinds of living. One was a recent victim of a C.P.R. accident. We chanced upon it in the morning paper, said how shocking it was and how perilous the lives of railway employees are, and forgot it with our rolls and coffee. But here lay the poor fellow whose memory is so much better than ours, the four or five line paragraph in actual, torn, bruised flesh and blood, still writhing in the horror of it, still trying to reconcile, through his glazed suffering eyes, this hospital world with the world he lived in five minutes before that awful crash and crush of falling earth from the wall of the tunnel that wrought thus with him four days ago. A broken back and arm and leg, and two or three ribs, one of the doctors said casually, a very bad case, that young Englishman's. But not so sad a one as this other's, who, by an accident in a manufactory, had lost both his arms almost at the sockets. Last year he helped himself merrily to his Christmas dinner; this year he is fed, as henceforth he must always be, by somebody else. Somebody else, too, wipes away the tears that run down his cheeks at the thought of his hard lot, of the mother whose only bread-winner he was, of the long years of his future dependence, for he is only nineteen. In perfectly sound bodily health, a man, with all the hope and energy and ambition that is common to men, he has to face a long existence helpless, hopeless.

Following in the gracious wake of Monseigneur we saw the other public wards and the private ones, which are very bright and cheerful, by the way, and should be well borne in mind by the possible victims of typhoid and other unpleasantnesses who may now be reading this chronicle. We saw the battery room, too, where all who so desire may freely partake of the electric fluid in unlimited quantity. And the kitchen where all the baking and broiling is done by gas, and all the boiling by steam. "In eight minutes," said one of the sisters to me, "we boiled yesterday one hundred and fifty gallons of soup." The dinner overhead was cooked in half-an-hour. Potatoes are boiled in three minutes for the whole establishment. By the wonderful steam apparatus in the laundry, three weeks washing is done, and dried, and ironed, all in one day, with the cooperation of one man and one servant. It was enough to turn the complexion of the private and secular housekeeper green with envy.

These things are not paid for yet by I think twenty thousand dollars. They are recent improvements and expensive. The hospital gets along nobly on its two thousand a year from the Provincial Government, its ninety cents a day per sailor from Ottawa, its revenue from private wards, and on the charity of the well and well-disposed of Montreal. But it will be apparent that this is not all sufficient for modern improvements. And so, among other plans to raise the money, there is to be a Kermesse on a very grand scale in June. Without waiting for this, however, I should suggest that any centenarians who are thinking of making their wills, or any able-bodied millionaires with a fancy for building their own monuments, should go and see Notre Dame Hospital by way of utilizing ready-made opportunities.

Montreal *Star*, December 30, 1887.

## Women's Medical College

I was reminded the other day that "Bric-a-brac" had apparently forgotten to supply its readers with information duly promised regarding the Women's Medical College at Kingston. If I am not mistaken, Tiglath-pileser interrupted us. Tiglath-pileser is opposed to the medical education of women, and when confronted with this unpardonable impoliteness, he declined to express any contrition whatever. In his opinion, the young woman of this generation does enough mischief now, without being licensed to do more. But Tiglath-pileser, since his experience in Bohemia, is by nature and occupation a cynic.

The Medical College for Women in Kingston is conducted very much as other colleges with the same object. It differs from that of Toronto in government insomuch as its governing board is appointed by its subscribers. This secures for the college the distinct advantage of having its affairs conducted by a body of men and women thoroughly, cordially and actively in sympathy with its every effort and most anxious to exert themselves on its behalf....

The lecture-rooms are at present located in the Kingston City Hall, where there is abundant and convenient accommodation for the present number of students. They are very neat and orderly, contrary to the traditions of medical lecture-rooms, and contained, when I saw them, not one thing that might properly be called a horror. I suppose there must be horrors occasionally, but they were very feebly represented in the physiological charts that hung on the wall, the little, coloured, self-developing dummy that reposed in a case, and the anatomical gentleman who swung amiably from a hook in the corner, very much bleached with the uses of adversity. Talking of horrors, of course I made the usual enquiries about the effect of the dissecting room upon feminine nerves. One of the students confessed that at first it was a little dreadful, but that very soon the natural repulsion to the work gave place to interest which grew until it became fascination, so wonderful and absorbing is the study of the complexities whereby we live and breathe and move and have our being. People are fond of saying that a certain feminine quality indescribable and impalpable as the bloom on the grape—that inevitable simile—must necessarily be lost in this process. I will believe it so far as to agree that it is apt to be. The influences which go to make the medical student of the other sex the graceless individual he is forgiven for being during the time of his probation cannot be wholly without effect upon his more susceptible sister. But it is quite possible, I think, that she may enter her course fully conscious of this, and defend herself against it. She may take all her little feminine instincts and administer an anaesthetic to them, wrap them up carefully in cotton wool, and put them away in some cerebral corner for the four years. With proper care and attention during the interval, they ought to be as good as new at the end of it.

There are twenty-five students at the Kingston College this year, in all stages of development. There are several distinct types among them, as naturally there would be among so many girls possessing logic and resolution and purpose enough to make M.D.s of themselves. Logic and resolution and purpose are not distinctively feminine qualities you are thinking, Monsieur? They used not to be, but nothing in this nineteenth century fever period of transition is more noticeable than the change it has brought to the women who live in it. It is still to be hoped, however, that we can restrain ourselves from filling civic positions with more profit than glory, from Amazonian behaviour, from wearing divided skirts, even from reading the newspaper at the breakfast table. Perhaps logic enough to remedy our former delightful but dismaying unreasonableness, resolution enough to prop up the feebleness of will that has always distinguished us so charmingly, and purpose enough to give aim and direction to lives that were once so actively and usefully spent in crocheting bead purses for charity fairs, would not be such a bad addition to our mental and moral capital after all.

Some of these young ladies are obtaining their medical training by their own efforts—"teaching themselves through" just as their brothers might do. Others are receiving it from parents who can afford to give their girls as fair odds in the struggle of life as they have given their boys. And there is more than one among the number who has preferred hard work of a student's life to certain social pleasures and distinctions that are quite enough for the life-long aim of many people. I believe six hundred dollars comfortably covers the expenses of the entire course. The students average much younger apparently than their brother medicos, whose regard for them is said to be now really fraternal....

Montreal *Star*, January 28, 1888.

### A Salvation Army Meeting

The Salvation Army is in some ways less conspicuous than it was in Calcutta, as in other parts of the worlds. Its leaders have learned the virtue of moderation and adaptability to other circumstances beside those of native life. Nowadays the big drum that reposes, when it does repose, in that lower flat in Bentinck Street, which is the army headquarters in Calcutta, no longer beats in the thick of the thoroughfares or in the midst of fashionable promenades, but is heard in shady squares and in streets less patronized by the hurrying broker or the restive pair in the breakers' van from Cook's or Hart's or Milton's. Nor is strict imitation of the native's dress, which was at first exacted, any more allowed. The lady "officer" with whom I had a little chat lately about the Army, was dressed in a white blouse and a dark skirt, with shoes on her feet and a sola topi on her head, her only distinguishing garment being the blue and white sari, which she wore draped over one shoulder, and the badge at her neck, which announced in silver letters, "Jesus is Mine." A few years ago, she might have been bare-footed and bare-headed; indeed in that guise she had at one time sold the *War Cry* in the New Market, and suffered very much from headache in consequence. But now, for Calcutta at least, that rule is wisely relaxed, though "up-country" as she enthusiastically told me, "the officers live exactly like the people, eat their food, do their own cooking and washing, and bathe at the ghats with the natives." The conditions of the work up-country evidently appealed to her as more whole-souled; the compromises of the capital had to be accepted, but they were less ideal. For the purposes of this article, I will call the lady Captain Brown. She was not a captain, and her name was not Brown, but that does not affect anything that she said or I saw.

> "I've got a Saviour that's mighty to keep
>    All day on Sunday and six days a week
> I've got a Saviour that's mighty to keep
>    Fifty-two weeks in the year."

It was very cheerful, very invigorating. From his frame high up on the wall, the "General" seemed to look down approvingly. Captain Brown was singing, and her lieutenant and one or two officers of both sexes, seven or eight men from the Fort, and four or five men from the Strand. Item, one pretty and modest-looking East Indian girl with her mother; item, one Savannah negro who enjoyed it more than anybody; item, one Chinaman, a figure in blue drill, an old ivory, only his eyes awake. They sang it again and again, the big drum keeping joyous time, Captain Brown and the lieutenant ringing in the tambourine. They sang other things, too, and always there was praying in between—praying which never mentioned the Queen or the Royal Family, but which told the Lord about the long voyage the "May Queen" or the "Mary Bell" was about to make, and humbly asked that all aboard her might be kept as straight as possible to their journey's end. Then Captain Brown said the meeting was "open for testimony," and first those who had been a long time saved got up and said so to encourage the others, and then a Danish soldier found his feet, and looked straight at the top of the door and said, "I suppose I sdop by Jesus—long time I suppose I sdop by Jesus." He didn't know how to go on, so Captain Brown smiled kindly and started another hymn. And then a Shropshire man got up. You could see by the clearness of his skin and his eyes that he belonged to the best class of the "Widow's" regimental property. He said he was happy and satisfied, and he looked it. He also said that though he never expected that those "here tonight" would ever meet again, he hoped, for his part, that they would all meet him in another and a better place which I will not particularize as he did, since it might look irreverent in a newspaper. Very simple sentiments, but it is easy to hear more elaborate ones on any road leading to the Fort of an evening, which are not so good for the ears.

I will not dwell on the testimonies—they might give occasion to the enemy to offend if they were transcribed....

*Indian Daily News*, December 1, 1896.

# VI    Literature

**Introduction**

The assertion made in the first sentence of this section ("literature is the noblest product of civilization") governs all of Sara Jeannette Duncan's writing on cultural subjects. She was never in doubt about the value of the vocation to which she had committed herself.

The same article, written in Washington for an American audience, anticipates her views on Canadian nationalism. "National literature cannot be wholly evolved from within," she told readers of the Washington *Post*, and almost two years later, she argued that "literary work that is bought and sold at an added consideration because it is Canadian is stamped with a meretricious value" ("Dangers of Literary Nationalism").

Yet Sara Jeannette Duncan was always eager to applaud and encourage Canadian writing when no sacrifices in critical judgment were required; sometimes she even let her loyalty get the better of her judgment. Her review of *An Algonquin Maiden* is a fascinating instance of an internal struggle between the competing claims of patriotism and literary standards. *An Algonquin Maiden* is an old-fashioned romance of the kind Sara Jeannette Duncan was inclined to regard with contempt (see "Outworn Literary Methods"). One suspects that only its Canadian authorship prompted her to launch into a defence of romance as a literary form.

"Colonialism and Literature" is such a masterly piece of cultural analysis that commentary on it is superfluous. Apart from the validity of its conclusions, it is a brilliantly argued essay. "American Influence on Canadian Thought," taken together with "Colonialism and Literature" and "Dangers of Literary Nationalism," shows Sara Jeannette Duncan's awareness of the three perils to which the struggling, incipient Canadian culture was exposed: excessive colonial humility, the cultural dominance of the United States and (in reaction to the first two factors), aggressive parochialism. In "International Copyright," Miss Duncan argues that foreign influence on a national literature is healthy; in "American Influence on Canadian Thought," she acknowledges that excessive foreign influence from one source can be dangerous.

Sara Jeannette Duncan is at her best as an analyst of cultural forces, and their social context. As a critic of individual literary works, she is often less persuasive. Yet she had an instinct for recognizing outstanding literary talent, even if she did not always have the critical vocabulary to articulate her enthusiasm. James's *The Bostonians* was attacked by most critics when it first appeared, and Conrad's *An Outcast of the Islands* was the work of an unknown writer. But Sara Jeannette Duncan was sympathetic to both works, and capable of defining at least some of their permanent qualities. She also took writers seriously enough to be influenced by them. Her reading of James may have resulted in the stylistic obscurity that marks the novels she wrote in the middle of her career; she also began to write more daringly about "the unspeakable things of life" shortly after she praised Conrad for his "marvellous power" with such material.

## International Copyright

....It will not be questioned that literature is the noblest product of civilization. That, first, civilized men made letters, and that then letters made civilized men, is historically true. The state of a nation's literature is the surest test of its advancement, but literature is not only the measure of a people's progress, it is also the means of their further advancement. Nothing, therefore, can be of more value to a people—nothing of more importance to a nation—than its literary products. Whatever promotes literary activity and elevates its sphere is a means of public benefit. The production of books therefore has direct relations to the public good.

But national literature cannot be wholly evolved from within. In the republic of letters the several domains are inter-dependent. A literature should have its roots in the national character and within national limits, and it should be, so to speak, racy of its native soil. But to give it growth, variety and comprehensive character, it has to be fed from without. The general current of human thought, as precipitated in literary forms, must be welcomed from all sources to preserve its vitality and promote its maturity. A national literature, shut off from all other literatures, would weaken and die of starvation. It follows, therefore, that the contact of other literature with our own is beneficial, and the production of American books is helped and stimulated by the introduction of foreign books.

The two points on which the recognition of the reciprocal rights of authors is urged are the justice which awards a man remuneration for the use by us of the products of his skill, ingenuity and industry, and the benefit to result to American authors from admission to a larger and surer market. Much of the reading of the American people is and has been furnished through a system of literary piracy, which has robbed the author of the legitimate fruits of his toil. This system is contrary to the instincts, traditions and honorable sentiments of this people, and as a matter of unfair dealing it ought to be abandoned to preserve the respect to which the national character should be entitled.

But, in addition to the plea of justice for the foreign author, the piratical system should be abandoned because it is injurious to American literature. That it is in two ways. First, cheap literature tends to ruin American book publishing. No American books of any worth can be issued from the American press in competition with the cheap pirated editions of foreign books. Second, if there are no publishers there can be no authors. A publisher before the Senate Committee yesterday gave an instance of a work of fiction, one of the best issued last season, which resulted in a loss, simply because the piratical competition is ruining the book trade.

The whole question is now being presented to Congress in good shape. The testimony of the most eminent American authors and publishers is being obtained, and there is a better prospect than ever before that Congressional indifference will be overcome, that considerations of reason and justice will prevail, and that a reciprocal copyright law will be passed.

Washington *Post*, January 29, 1886.

**The Bostonians**

Mr. Henry James' most elaborate achievement has appeared. One's first impression is that it has appeared very hideously. Its bulky personality is done up in plain cloth of terra cotta hue, and looks precisely like a "Handy Hand-Book," or a volume from a circulating library, or a red brick....

The first page of Mr. James' writing, however, overwhelms one with a conviction that criticism of its exterior is rather a graceless task. The pleasure it affords is so perfect of its kind, and its kind is so distinctive and so rare.

"The Bostonians" is a novel founded on the social aspects of the "woman question," if its peculiarly airy and fantastic architecture can be properly said to have any foundation at all. The story may be told in three lines. An enthusiastic young suffragist, who is rich, meets another who is poor and pretty and eloquent, exploits her in the cause, wraps around her the invincible mantle of her own stern antipathy to the genus man and the state of matrimony, and is as dismally happy as one may be under such circumstances in Boston. Then a Mississippian cousin appears and begins to spoil the situation by making love to her *protegée*. This young man has no "views" to speak of concerning woman, except that she should be adorable and adored. So he continues to spoil the situation until he positively ruins it by running away with the pretty orator on the very eve of an occasion on which her efforts would undoubtedly have convinced the whole of Boston. That is all.

As to the *motif* of the book, we can hardly think it is seriously meant as a contribution of Mr. James' views upon the social question which forms its theme. If it is so to be considered, it is certainly the work of a man with a very bitter prejudice and very narrow vision. A fair picture of the movement could hardly fail to deprecate it, but this is a caricature. There is no dealing with the features of the subject; Mr. James does not condescend to that. He is in no sense an essayist anyway, and least of all in his novels. His artistic perception is too keen and sure to permit discussion where there is room for depiction only. But the role of ridicule in which he attires the unhappy leaders of the agitation is so indiscriminate in its fashion as to lead one to the conclusion that Mr. James' fancy was caught by the novel possibilities of his subject, and that he subordinated all considerations of fidelity and justice to the effective elaboration of its entertaining phases.

If one is careful not to regard them too typically, however, these latest published creations of Mr. James are among the most delightful for which we are yet indebted to him. Verena Tarrant, the young lady with the gift of speech, a highly nervous organization and glowing enthusiasm regarding the liberation of her sex from what she is firmly impressed is their present condition of bondage, is a genuine "find." She has no parallel in fiction. She is fresh, delightfully real, by all odds the most vivifying influence that Mr. James has yet put into his work. This novelist has a habit, not wholly to be condemned, since he does it so well, of regarding humanity from a strictly anthropologic standpoint and of tabulating the peculiarities of individual specimens with rather less sympathy than is displayed by the average collector of beetles. This young lady marks a distinct advance toward the more ordinary methods of fiction....

It would be difficult, however, for Mr. James to bring any feature into his books that would surpass their single charm of style. This author has not really so very much to say; but he has such a delightfully incisive way of saying it that one forgets the comparative insignificance of his subject in the art with which he presents it. His idea may be infinitesimal, but the polished dexterity with which he handles it occupies an intellectual expanse that crude, strong thought might barely fill. Mr. James permits this clever manipulation of his very frequently to run away with him. Very notably he has done so in this book of Boston. It will be found much too long by everybody to whom the exquisite refinement of his expression and the consummate art of his treatment does not bring a keen intellectual pleasure entirely apart from his subject....But the few who do not find it the easiest matter to get too much of a good thing will read every line of "The Bostonians" with a sense of enjoyment that modern fiction imparts with sad infrequency.

Washington *Post*, April 4, 1886.


**Colonialism and Literature**


We are still an eminently unliterary people.

Another Canadian summer has waxed and waned; mysterious in our forests, idyllic in our gardens, ineffably gracious upon our mountains. Another year of our national existence has rounded into the golden fulness of its harvest time. The yellow leaves of another September are blowing about our streets; since last we watched their harlequin dance to dusty death a

cycle has come and gone. And still the exercise of hope and faith
—charity we never had—continue to constitute the sum of
our literary endeavour. We are conscious of not having been
born in time to produce an epic poet or a dramatist; but still in
vain do we scan the west for the lyrist, the east for the novelist
whose appearing we may not unreasonably expect. Our bard is
still loath to leave his Olympian pleasures; our artisan in fiction
is busy with the human product of some other sphere.

And we look blankly at each other at every new and vain
adjustment of the telescope to the barren literary horizon, and
question "Why?" And our American cousins with an indifferent
wonder, and a curious glance at our census returns, make the
same interrogatory; whereupon one of them tarries in Montreal
for three days, ascertains, and prints in *Harper's Magazine* that
it is our arctic temperature! And in England, if our sterile
national library excites any comment at all, it is only a semi-
contemptuous opinion that it is all that might be expected of
"colonials."

Mr. Warner's idea that the Canadian climate reduces the
Canadian brain to a condition of torpor during the six months
of the year may be dismissed with something of the irritation
which it inspired in every Canadian who read it, that a writer
who observes so keenly in his own country could be led to such
an absurd and superficial conclusion in ours. One would
naturally suppose that climatic influences which produce the
bodily results to be found in the average Canadian, at least
conduce toward giving him an active mind as well. Physically,
Canadians compare with Americans to the great disadvantage
of the latter; that they do not intellectually, alas! is not the
fault of the climate.

Nor can we place the slightest responsibility for our literary
short-comings upon our educational system. On the contrary,
our colleges and public schools are our pride and glory. We
point boastfully to the opportunities for intellectual elevation
Ontario offers to the children of her navvies and farm labourers;
and the ease with which Canadian graduates obtain all sorts of
American degrees testifies to the thoroughness of our university
training. So great indeed are our facilities for education that our
farm lands lie untilled while our offices are filled to unprofitable
repletion, and grave protest is arising in many quarters against
the State's present liberal abetment of this false adjustment of
national energy to national needs. Clearly, Nature and the Hon.
G.W. Ross can do no more for us. We are a well-developed and

well-educated people; but we do not write books.

"No, for we are not rich enough," you say. "The cultivation of letters demands wealth and a leisure class. We have a professional market in view for our hard-bought college training. We cannot afford to offer it up in unremunerative libations to the muses. We choose between the rustic homespun and the academic bombasin, but there the alternative ends. It is hard work thenceforward in either case. For Canadians to 'sport with Amaryllis in the shade, or with the tangles of Neraea's hair' is an idyllic occupation which, for financial reasons, must be sternly ignored."

This is a comfortable way of relegating the responsibility for our literary inactivity to an economic dispensation of an overruling Providence which finds favour with a great many people. The disabilities of poverty are so easy to assume! But the theory is too plausible to be tenable. A wealthy public is necessary perhaps to the existence of authors who shall also be capitalists. A leisure class is a valuable stimulus to literary production. But money and the moneyed can neither command nor forbid the divine afflatus. The literary work produced solely by hope of gain is not much of an honour to any country. While authorship is a profession with pecuniary rewards like any other, those who are truly called to it obey a law far higher than that of demand and supply. Genius has always worked in poverty and obscurity; but we never find it withdrawing from its divinely appointed labour, and taking to law or merchandise on that account. When the great Canadian *litterateur* recognises himself he will not pause to weigh the possibilities of Canada's literary market before he writes the novel or the poem that is to redeem our literary reputation. Let genius be declared amongst us, and the market may be relied upon to adjust itself to the marvellous circumstance, for a great deal of the talk of Canadian poverty is the veriest nonsense. Riches are relative. We have no bonanza kings; but our railroad magnates are comfortably, not to say luxuriously, housed and horsed and apparelled. We work hard, but the soil is grateful; we are not compelled to struggle for existence. The privations of our Loyalist forefathers do not survive in us. We are well fed, well clad, well read. Why should we not buy our own books!

We would buy them if they were written. That they are not written is partly our own fault and partly that of circumstances. We cannot compel the divine afflatus; but we can place ourselves in an attitude to receive that psychical subtlety should the gods deign to bestow it upon us. But the Olympians, bending Canada-ward, hear no prayer for their great guerdons. We are indifferent; we go about our business and boast of the practical nature of our aspirations; we have neither time nor the inclination for star-gazing, we say. The Province of Ontario is one great camp of the Philistines.

Apart from the necessarily untrustworthy testimony of one's own more or less limited acquaintance, there is but one proof of this—the newspapers; and in a free and enlightened country there is no better exponent of the character of the people than the character of its press. The influence of the daily newspaper is not greater than the influence of public opinion upon the daily newpaper. In a very great measure we dictate what manner of editorial we shall take with our coffee; and either of our great morning dailies is eloquent of our tastes. Politics and vituperation, temperance and vituperation, religion and vituperation; these three dietetic articles, the vituperative sauce invariably accompanying, form the exclusive journalistic pabulum of three-quarters of the people of Ontario. No social topics of other than a merely local interest, no scientific, artistic, or literary discussions, no broad consideration of matters of national interest—nothing but perpetual jeering, misconstruction, and misrepresentation for party ends of matters within an almost inconceivably narrow range.

"Why do you print no book reviews?" I asked the editor of a leading journal recently.

"People don't care about them, and it interfered with advertising," was his truly Philistinish response. And the first reason must have a certain amount of truth in it; for if it were not so, public spirit would never tolerate the withholding of such matter for the contemptible—in this connection—consideration of "advertising." Our French compatriots have not this spirit. But they have their Frechette and their Garneau.

A spirit of depreciation of such faint stirrings of literary life as we have amongst us at present has often been remarked in Canadians, a tendency to nip forth-putting buds by contemptuous comparison with the full blown production of other lands, where conditions are more favourable to literary efflorescence. This is a distinctly colonial trait; and in our character as colonists we find the root of all our sins of omission in letters. "In the political life of a colony," writes one of us in the New York *Critic*, "there is nothing to fire the imagination, nothing to arouse enthusiasm, nothing to appeal to national pride." Our enforced political humility is the distinguishing characteristic of every phase of our national life. We are ignored, and we ignore ourselves. A nation's development is like a plant's, unattractive under ground. So long as Canada remains in political obscurity, content to thrive only at the roots, so long will the leaves and blossoms of art and literature be scanty and stunted products of our national energy. We are swayed by no patriotic sentiment that might unite our diverse provincial interests in the common cause of our country. Our politics are a game of grab. At stated intervals our school children sing with great gusto, "The Maple Leaf Forever!" but before reaching man's estate, they discover that it is only the provincial variety of maple leaf vegetation that they may reasonably be expected to toast. Even civil bloodshed in Canada has no dignity, but takes the form of inter-provincial squabbling. A national literature cannot be looked for as an outcome of anything less than a complete national existence.

Of course we have done something since we received our present imperfect autonomy in 1867. We have our historians, our essayists, and our chirping poets. And in due time, we are told, if we have but faith and patience, Canadian literature will shine as a star in the firmament. Meanwhile, however, we are uncomfortably reminded of that ancient and undisputed truism, "Faith without works is dead."

*The Week*, September 30, 1886.

## An Algonquin Maiden

The publication of a Canadian work of poetry or fiction, or any of the lighter arts of literature, by a Canadian firm, among Canadians, is apt to be received with peculiar demonstrations. Their facial form is that of an elongation of the countenance, a pursing of the lips, a lifting of the eyebrows. This is usually accompanied by a little significant movement of the shoulders which we have borrowed from our French-Canadian relations-in-law expressly for use in this regard. We pick up the unfortunate volume from the bookseller's counter to which its too trustful author has confided it, and we turn its leaves in a manner we reserve for Canadian publications—a manner that

109

expresses curiosity rather than a desire to know, and yet one that is somehow indicative of a foregone conclusion....

How futile is the attempt to make broad highways in any department of literature, and say dictatorially to them that travel in that direction "Walk therein"!....This is especially true of fiction, the art of which, having for its shifting and variable basis, humanity, is bound to present itself in more diverse forms than any other...Yet in fiction, rather more than anywhere else, are autocrats to be found, who announce to their scribbling emulators the only proper and acceptable form of the modern novel, announce it imperiously, and note departures from it with wrath. Hardly more months than one could reckon on one's fingers, and hardly years enough to reckon at all, have gone by since we became familiar with the principles and practice of the realistic school, for instance....Gentlemen of the realistic school, one is disposed to consider you very right in so far as you go, but to believe you mistaken in your idea that you go the whole distance and can persuade the whole novel-writing fraternity to take the same path through the burdocks and the briars. Failing this, you evidently believe that you can put to the edge of the sword every wretched romancist who presumes to admire the ideal of the exotic and to publish his admiration. This also is a mistake, for both of the authors of "An Algonquin Maiden" are alive, and, I believe, in reasonable health; and "An Algonquin Maiden" is a romance, a romance of the most uncompromising description, a romance that might have been written if the realistic school had never been heard of. One need go no further than the title to discover it a romance; "maidens" are unknown to the literary methods of a later date. They have become extinct, and are less euphonically replaced. Even in poetry usage has handed the word over to be, along with his coronet, the exclusive literary property of Lord Tennyson. More than this, the title boldly states, as well as implies, the character of the book. "A Romance," its authors have had the temerity to sub-title it, "of the Early Days of Upper Canada." This must be regarded as nothing less than a challenge to the modern idea of the form of latter-day fiction. One hardly knows whether most to admire the courage that inspired it, or to depre-cate the reckless disregard for consequences that sent it forth into a world too apt, as we all know, to be unduly influenced by the opinion of the majority. But we cannot pause too long in this emotional vacillation. The fact is accomplished, published, and in all the bookstores; let us consider the fact.

"An Algonquin Maiden" is the beautiful foster-daughter of an old Indian chief. Her name is Wanda. She probably had another name, but the authors have mercifully left us in ignorance of it. The necessary struggle with the polysyllabic nomenclature of the noble red man has never yet been sufficiently considered among the facts inimical to Canadian immigration. Wanda is a sort of familiar in the household of Colonel Macleod, whose son Edward makes her the object of somewhat less than one-half of his divided affections. Edward has a sister Rose, a bright, sprightly, charming little damsel, whose character is said to be an easily recognisable portrait. Rose is in love with one Allan Dunlop, a sturdy young Candian Reformer, who reciprocates, but somewhat hopelessly, he believes, on account of the political opinions of the gentleman he is anxious to make his parent-in-law, who is a Tory of a type that can only be called cerulean. The remaining character of importance to the working out of the story is Mdlle. Hélène de Berczy, the rival of the Algonquin maiden for the somewhat unstable and irresponsible affections of Mr. Edward Macleod. The story runs naturally and easily through various stages in the affairs of these young people, in which jealousy plays an important emotional part, and the chief incident is an accident to the piquant little Rose, by which she is romantically shut up for some days in the old stone farm house of her Reformer lover, who adds bucolics to politics in his worthy career. True to the traditions of romance, the authors arrange a perfectly satisfactory termination of affairs for everybody concerned. Odd numbers being incompatible with unalloyed bliss, Miss Wetherald drowns the unfortunate Algonquin maiden, in the chapter before the last, which she styles poetically "The Passing of Wanda"—drowns her in a passage of such sympathetic grace that one becomes more than reconciled to the sad necessity of the act, and convinced that the love-smitten Algonquin maiden herself could ask no happier fate.

....We are much interested in the Indian annals and legends to which we are introduced by the way; yet the carping critic in us cries out at the idea of putting them in the mouth of an Algonquin chief in such grandiloquent manner as this:

By its clear light they saw, far in the distance, two strange, enormous things moving towards them. But whether these things were writhing wreaths of thunderclouds descended to earth, or gigantic trees denuded

111

of their foliage and suddenly gifted with the power of motion, or whether they were wild beasts of a size never seen before, they could not tell.

If this is a genuine product of the aboriginal intelligence fifty years ago, one is moved to tears at the thought of its degeneration under the vitiating influences of modern civilisation since.

Mr. Adam's hand is easy to detect in the book. He does not romance. He will be doubtless equally guilty in the eyes of the realistic host with Miss Wetherald in supplying the facts upon which the romance is based; but we do not catch him *in flagrante delicto* anywhere. He does not allude to the Macleods' man-of-all-work as "the ancient servitor," to Edward Macleod as "the young master of Pine Towers," or to Miss de Berczy as "the lovely Helene," and Miss Wetherald does. Nor does he anywhere stand confessed in such a sentence as:

Edward rose and beheld in the open doorway Helene de Berczy; her large glance, darker than a thundercloud, was illumined by a long lightning flash of merciless irony.

As Edward had been kissing the Algonquin maiden, one cannot help feeling that this was precisely what he deserved; yet it is retribution which evokes a certain pity.

To return to Mr. Adam, it is impossible to help wishing that his guiding and restraining hand were evident upon more pages of "An Algonquin Maiden" than it is. Where he assists in the character portraiture, the result is much more satisfactory than Miss Wetherald's unaided creations, delicate and graceful though some of these may be. Allan Dunlop is decidedly the strongest individual in the book, and he owes most of his personality to Mr. Adam. The historical and political parts of the volume, which form by no means too much ballast for Miss Wetherald's more aerial writing, we owe entirely to Mr. Adam; and it will probably be wished in many quarters that we had been given more chapters like that upon "Politics at the Capital," even at the expense of a few of the sort of that upon "A Kiss and its Consequences"....

*The Week*, January 13, 1887.

....Vastly changed, too, is the literature of travel. The spirit of modern art has entered into it, and we get broad effects, strong lights, massed shadows in our foreign picture, and ready impressions from it. The process of eternal word-stippling has gone out of favour. It does not take three pages for an adequate presentation of a Swiss sunset now; and to print the emotions inspired by it is considered, providentially for the public, out of date. We have had one Ruskin, who painted as he chose and what he chose, from the tiny gray-green mountain lichen to the torrent that rushed past it, and in all things made us gladly worshipful of the genius that wielded his brush. The traveller of to-day either recognises that the climax of the art has been reached, and mercifully forbears effort, or is persuaded by his publisher that the meditations of the ordinary mind upon mountain scenery are a drug in the market. And so he turns from the old painstaking chronicle of them, supplemented by the information in his Baedeker, and such historical association as has filtered through the years since he left school, and writes graphically instead of the humanity about him, its tricks of speech, its manner of breaking bread, its ideals, aims, superstitions....

In fiction, that literary department that knows only the limits of human nature, there is the greatest change. All orthodoxy is gone out of it. It does not matter in the least whether there is a heroine or not, and if there is her ultimate fate is of no consequence whatever. To the casual observer little order or method seems to prevail in the set of circumstances taken apparently at random from anybody's experience, and cut off at both ends to suit the capacity of the cover. But in this respect appearances are deceitful. The novel of to-day may be written to show the culminative action of a passion, to work out an ethical problem of every-day occurrence, to give body and form to a sensation of the finest or of the coarsest kind, for almost any reason which can be shown to have a connection with the course of human life, and the development of human character. Motives of this sort are not confined to any given school or its leaders, but affect the mass of modern novel writers very generally, and inspire all whose work rises above the purpose of charming the idle hour of that bored belle in her boudoir, whose taste used to be so exclusively catered to by the small people in fiction. The old rules by which any habitual novel reader could prophesy truly at the third chapter how the story would "come out" are disregarded, the well-worn incidents discarded, the *sine qua nons* audaciously done without. Fiction has become a law unto itself, and its field has broadened with the assumption.

The practical spirit of the age has subtler, farther-reaching influences than we dream of. It requires simplicity in the art of the pen for readier apprehension in a busy time. Even the sciences appear divested of their old formalism and swagger. It demands sensation by the shortest nerve route. It has decided for light upon some practical subjects through plain window panes to the partial exclusion of stained glass embellished with saints and symbols. It asks, in short, that adaptation of method to matter which is so obscure yet so important a factor in all literary work.

*The Week*, June 9, 1887.


## American Influence on Canadian Thought

....The future existence of Canada as a nation seems imperilled just now by the forces that lie behind a grave doubt. The future existence of a Canadian national literature is not openly threatened, but it is none the less in danger. In fact the influences assailing literary effort here have nothing to do with the blandishments of the Annexationists. If Canada becomes part of the Union in the very infancy of her literature, of course it will grow to the full stature of an American; but even if she does not, it is greatly to be feared that the offspring of her brain may show more than cousinship for its relations over the border. More than one generation of people who talked of England or Scotland or Ireland as "home," people of refinement, scholarly tastes, and a certain amount of leisure have taken in hand the construction of a Canadian literature. Their ideals were British, their methods were British, their markets were chiefly British, and they are mostly gathered to their British fathers, leaving the work to descendants, whose present, and not whose past, country is the actual, potential fact in their national life. There is a wide difference, though comparatively few years span it, between a colonial and a Canadian, and we may not unnaturally look for a corresponding difference in their literary productions. That the difference will be, for a long time at least, not perceptible as between British and Canadian, but rather as between British and American, may be expected for several reasons.

The most obvious of these is perhaps the great number of American books and magazines that find ready readers here. The literary faculty is more imitative than any other, especially in the earlier stages of its endeavour, and it is prone to imitate first in the direction of its own liking. This direction may be readily guessed at by a comparison of the number of English and American contemporary writers familiar to the present generation of Canadian readers, by which the latter will be found to preponderate in almost anybody's experience. If this is in the nature of an impression, and therefore indefinite, let us ask the City Librarian how they stand in popularity, and he will doubtless put the impression in figures—clothe it with the unanswerable logic of a statistic. Any bookseller in the city will tell us that for one reader of Blackmore or Meredith he finds ten of Howells or James; any book reviewer will testify to the largely American sources from which the volumes of his praise or objurgation come; any newsdealer will give us startling facts as to the comparative circulation of the American and the English magazines, and if he be a Toronto newsdealer may add a significant word or two about the large sale in this city of the Buffalo *Sunday Express*. There are still many colonials in this country, and lest they, with their families, should feel stigmatised by the foregoing statement, we hasten to except them. For the most part they stick to the traditions of their youth, their English classics, and their *Weekly Times*; and Frank Harris's *Fortnightly* is as necessary to their happiness as English breakfast tea. It is not true of them that they are partial to American writers. If you speak to them of the fiction of that great country, they reply by a reference to Fenimore Cooper, which shows the subject to be so unpromising that you change it. But of the mass of Canadians it is true. It is not, however, the taste or the literary culture implied in the fact, but the fact itself that is pertinent to our argument. Once Canadian minds are thoroughly impregnated with American matter, American methods, in their own work, will not be hard to trace.

It is pertinent here to consider the difference in the price of English and American publications, which is great, and doubtless often induces the book-buyer to choose the lesser good at the cheaper rate. The English publisher finds it to his interest to bring out a first edition of an average successful novel at 31s. 6d. His American brother knows it to be very remunerative to publish a book of the same class at $1.50. The same duty on both books makes the price to the Canadian thirty per cent higher. He buys the American book in part because it is the cheapest, but in greater part because he is in every respect the sort of person whose existence in great numbers in the United States makes its publication profitable. The lack of moneyed leisure is not the only condition of life common to Americans and Canadians. If it were, American literature would be as impotent, at any price, to change the character of Canadian literature as it is to effect a literary revolution in England. But, like the Americans, we have a certain untrammelled consciousness of new conditions and their opportunities, in art as well as in society, in commerce, in government. Like them, having a brief past as a people, we concentrate the larger share of thought, energy, and purpose upon our future. We have their volatile character, as we would have had without contact with them; volatility springs in a new country as naturally as weeds. We have greatly their likings and their dislikings, their ideas and their opinions. In short, we have not escaped, as it was impossible we should escape, the superior influence of a people overwhelming in numbers, prosperous in business, and aggressive in political and social faith, the natural conditions of whose life we share, and with whom we are brought every day into closer contact....

*The Week*, July 7, 1887.

**Dangers of Literary Nationalism**

Mr. G. Mercer Adam has a very interesting article in a recent number of *The Week*. It is called "Nationalism and the Literary Spirit," and to those who know Mr. Adam's oft-expressed, kindly and enthusiastic views upon the subject of Canadian literature its conclusions will be foregone. For the benefit of those who do not know them it may be said that Mr. Adam considers it the duty of the national spirit to nourish the literary spirit. He believes that the Canadian author should be encouraged by Canadians. Mr. Adam's phrase is classic and I should not attempt to paraphrase it, but I think he finds the depression in Canadian letters due mainly to the fact that we do not, as a rule, buy the publications of our native land and devote our time and attention to endeavouring to be pleased or profited by them because they are native....

It would be pleasant to agree with Mr. Adam. His theory would shed a cheerful and optimistic light upon the situation. If, by reason of neglect only, and indifference and that unpleasant anatomical portion known as the "cold shoulder," Canadian literature has failed to reach the full stature of its possibilities, then surely all that is wanted to develop it is liberal and discriminating patronage....

It is in reality the most unkind thing possible to place a meretricious value upon work of any sort, and literary work that is bought and sold at an added consideration because it is Canadian is stamped with a meretricious value. We do, I think, a mistaken thing every time we buy a book we do not want for any other reason simply for this one. Gold is gold all over the world, and the literary standard should be equally unalterable. If not, the inferior metal we pretend to appraise at the same value because it was mined in our own country will be certain one day to be tried as by fire, with disastrous results.

We may safely say that now-a-days the measure of the worth of a book determines its fate nearly always. It is easy to cite notable instances in the past where this has not been the case; but in our age, with its great facilities for cheap production, enormous appetite for all that is produced, and keen competition in obtaining the wherewithal to gratify this appetite, there is very little chance of good work in any literary department failing of appreciation. The Canadian market may be a limited and unsatisfactory one for reasons quite beyond the reach of the writer, reasons, I mean, which his work does not affect; but there is nothing to show why he cannot take his wares to the English or the American publishing houses. He has already done this in some cases. And when he can compete successfully with workmen of his craft in England and the United States it will be his natural course. When this comes to pass Canadian work will not lack Canadian appreciation, not because it is stamped with British or American approval, but because, having reached a much more critical standard than any that has been established here it will necessarily be good work.

The fact is that our literary standards, if we have any, are much too low. Too much has always been taken into consideration in judging Canadian work—always leaving out what our scientists have done. Our colonial status, our comparative poverty, our youth, are allowed to plead for us when they all should be silent. We hear too often "It is very well, considering." Let it be very well, absolutely not relatively, or let it not be at all—at least let us not hear about it. Judgment is not passed on our cattle or our wheat with charity, nor payments made for them with liberality because they are "really better than might be expected," and the feeble efforts of a country three hundred years old ought to be "encouraged." Neither should criticisms of our books be made on that principle. Our tendancy to over-praise our own productions and to listen complacently while the *Spectator* or *Athenaeum* chucks us patronizingly under the chin and compliments us on our A.B.C's is working the destruction of a national literature; and instead of being fostered should be sternly repressed. A virile manifestation is beginning to be noticeable among the laborers in the literary field, a feeling of slight dissatisfaction with the reward of more candied than candid Canadian newspaper notices, supplemented by the gracious acknowledgment of a gilt-edged copy by His Excellency the Governor-General, who also thinks it his duty, doubtless, to "encourage" colonial efforts in this direction. The result will be that over-sensitive writers and it is a lamentable fact that many of the best writers are over-sensitive, will eschew the Canadian market altogether, or at least until after their work has passed a severer critical ordeal elsewhere. In proof of which I may say that a gentleman whose somewhat fitful and desultory court to the muses has already repaid him and many of his friends in the most delightful and original way, told me the other day that he meant to submit his MS. to English or to American publishers, failing the favorable verdict of whom he would not permit it to see the light at all. And this was not, I think, from fear of underappreciation, but of too ready and easy and meaningless overappreciation.

Montreal *Star*, January 31, 1888.

## An Outcast of the Islands

There are many things which the Imperial spirit, exulting in the power, the resource and the development of the rule of Great Britain, wherever the sun looks down, forgets to chronicle because of the abundance of more conspicuous matters to triumph over. Doubtless, they would be regarded by the Imperial spirit, which is quite the most admirably Philistine of British characteristics, as mere details of an impressive whole. They have to do with the art of living and with the other arts which are rapidly being colonialised; our necessarily brief reference this morning is especially to the art of literature. The last ten years have brought creditable romance and song from Australia; a whole band of poets and one or two novelists have arisen in Canada....The creative spirit has arisen in the far places of the earth where the English language is its medium... The necessary condition of life without anxiety and without penury have been established; and out of the tranquility that ensues art buds timidly, like a flower newly acclimitised.

Quite a wonderful instance of this is personified in Mr. Joseph Conrad...Up to the present we believe Mr. Conrad has published but two novels—*Almayer's Folly* and *An Outcast of the Islands*—and it has been our fortune to have seen the latter only. It is abundantly enough, however, to produce the conviction that a very powerful and original addition is made to the modern novelists in its author, who has chosen, by some whim of fate, a corner of the earth strangely remote even from India, at whose doors it lies, to reveal to us. The Dutch Straits Settlements might have been thought the last place to lend vivid material with the strongest psychological cast to the maker of fiction...and indeed, the reader's mind occupies itself before a dozen pages are turned with conjectures as to how so remarkable an intellect as the author's ever managed to find itself in intimate observation of warehouses of rubber and rattans and Arab traders and gubernatorial Sunday card parties at Batavia...as well as the intimate details of Malay life and character which abound throughout the book. It is rare enough to find the literary artificer in the world of Anglo-India, where the conditions are complex enough to produce him and society varied enough to be his orbit, but nothing short of astonishing when he appears in the Samarany Roads. To pass, however, from vague, and possibly impertinent surmise as to

Mr. Conrad himself, we must repeat that Mr. Conrad's novel is perhaps the very best sustained piece of work of the kind that has come out of the East. It concerns itself with the moral deterioration of a scoundrel, a clerk in a Dutch trading-house at Macassar, who falls under native influence, and particularly under that of his passion for a native woman....The material is therefore sordid enough, and difficult indeed of redemption from the utterly squalid and repellant; but Mr. Conrad possesses not inconsiderably the power of Zola and of Hardy, that marvellous power of transmuting the unspeakable things of life, with the effect that they are not only bearable upon the printed page, but serve undeniable ends of art....The life described has points of such similarity with that which obtains in the country of our own exile, that the author would be able at once to claim our corroboration, even if his pages were not full of that subtle and quite indescribable quality that attests the truth, to atmosphere, to colour, and to fact, of what he writes.

The book, in short, is one of great power and beauty....It speaks...of a great reserve of strength on the part of the author, which, if his observation of life be at all commensurate with it, should give us even greater things than *An Outcast of the Islands* from his pen. Not to omit the critical word, it might be said that the present novel dwells rather too continuously upon the high-strained note of the morbid consciousness, the effect being here and there after a time almost hysterical...The restful drop to common things and normal feelings does not come often enough. But this is in truth the defect of its quality, and it would be ungrateful to insist too much upon it....

*Indian Daily News*, October 12, 1896.